Resilien

CW01501860

Embracing Challenge and Change

by Will Hussey

'Hands down, the best book you'll read this decade.'

Dr Andy Cope
Author of *The Art of Being Brilliant*

Brilliant
PUBLICATIONS

About the author

This is the bit where Will tells you he's an international keynote thingumajig and a best-selling thingy. He's not going to do that, because hopefully the words in the book will speak for themselves. Suffice to say Will enjoys working with people far and wide to deliver positive, sustainable change for the better.

If you'd like to hear the words direct from the horse's mouth, feel free to drop him a line at will@willhussey.co.uk or subscribe to his newsletter via the QR code.

Brilliant Publications Limited
Unit 10
Sparrow Hall Farm
Edlesborough
Dunstable
Bedfordshire
LU6 2ES, UK

www.brilliantpublications.co.uk

Brilliant Publications is a registered trademark.

Written by Will Hussey
Illustrated by Isabella Valerio
Designed by Brilliant Publications Limited

© Brilliant Publications Limited 2024

Print ISBN: 978-1-78317-366-2
pdf ISBN: 978-1-78317-367-9

First printed and published in the UK in 2024

The right of Will Hussey to be identified as the author of this work has been asserted by himself in accordance with the Copyright, Designs and Patents Act 1988.

Contents

Foreword

Slowly
Slowly the seconds tick away,
Slowly the baby learns to play,
Slowly the days turn into a year,
Slowly the boy's questions become clear.

Slowly the years make up a decade,
Slowly youth's energy begins to fade,
Slowly the silver turns to grey,
Slowly, so slowly, life fades away.

By Tom Hussey, aged 12, 1982

Resilience 2.0 *was never intended to begin with an end, but in the midst of writing this book my father suddenly and unexpectedly passed away. All good things come to an end, and so it seems, do good people. Extraordinarily wonderful people.*

If he had his time again, I wonder if he'd choose to do anything differently? If.

As far as we're aware, none of us get to have our time again. But we do get to have our time. I'm not sure whether it's possible to make a fresh start, but a fresh middle is eminently possibly and, most definitely, a more promising future.

Maybe beginnings and ends are actually just bookends for the same thing. Life is just the filling, sandwiched in time. This book is about choice. You still have one. Choose your filling wisely.

For MKH: 1940 - 2022

Introduction

The trouble with history is just that: it's history. In the past. Apart from the recent trailer, none of us were actually around to experience the bigger picture. So, when we're told that times were tough years ago, it doesn't mean much. Sure, on some level we get it, but we don't really relate to it. We can only relate to our own experiences, i.e. now. And the truth is, that for many, life feels pretty tough right now. None of us really know whether it was better or worse in the 'good' old days, but I do know that the good old days have been and gone. What counts, is how you make the best of now.

Which is what this book is about. Making the best of now just so happens to involve making the very best of you. I'm not suggesting it's easy, but it is eminently doable. When the world's doing its worst, it's important to be something approaching your best. Which invariably requires upping your resilience.

This book is to resilience what self-raising flour is to baking. It's the single most important ingredient for elevating your existence from surviving to thriving, and regaining an appetite for life.

We look at the importance of perspective, and how 'looking' matters, but matter matters more. We all know that actions speak louder than words, but knowing it is not quite enough. Translating good intentions into great outcomes requires giving yourself a good talking to, and that's just for starters. Acknowledging our propensity to blame others for our predicament is key to accepting responsibility for change. Sure, things might get better, just like you might win the lottery. Your chances are significantly improved once you determine to make things happen rather than wait for things to happen.

Knowing what to do when you don't know what to do is key to embracing challenge and change. That's right: upping your resilience requires engaging with both. The bad news is that it's a rollercoaster ride. The good news is that it's a rollercoaster ride. Either way, it's non-negotiable, so strap yourself in. If only they taught you this at school. Fortunately, it's not too late. We never stop learning but might also benefit from a spot of unlearning.

Of course we're human beings not human *doings*; knowing what to do is only half the story. Harnessing resilience requires knowing how to 'be'.

In this book we'll explore five essential behaviours guaranteed to positively transform your relationship with the world – and yourself:

1. **Receptivity**. You've got be up for it.
2. **Risk**. Be prepared to brave it.
3. **Retention**. Stick at it.
4. **Responsibility**. Take accountability for it.
5. **Redefine**. Review your role in it.

Human beings are capable of amazing things if only we get out of our own way. These behaviours not only help you to stand back whilst simultaneously getting stuck in, but also give you a significant leg-up. As you can imagine, flexibility is key.

Confusing? It really isn't. With a little help from Indiana Jones, Han Solo and my five-year-old next-door neighbour (amongst others) this book is accessible, relatable and applicable to all. Life's far too short to do anything but live fully, completely and unapologetically.

Up your resilience and make the very best of it.

Chapter 1

Sleight of Head

Life is full on, isn't it?

No doubt, you've got a lot on several plates. Constantly spinning, simultaneously juggling, routinely picking up the pieces. Like many, you've become the clown in your very own circus, and it doesn't feel very funny.

People incessantly ask a lot, maybe even demand. Priorities, deadlines and urgent reminders abound.

You might have put up with an awful lot, already. More than your fair share. Your fair share probably doesn't feel very fair.

Who is this book for?

✱ Those who are tired of putting up with it: trying to make the best of a bad lot. For the exhausted, the disillusioned and those who, quite frankly, deserve better.

✱ The millions of people who are struggling with life: the basics, the baffling complexities and the contradictions. Struggling to make ends meet with the stratospherically soaring costs of living, struggling to work, or maybe struggling in work. Struggling in big ways, and struggling in smaller ways, struggling together, or struggling all alone. Struggling because everything feels oppressively the same, or struggling because they feel different.

✱ Those people for whom life is a constant battle of attrition, continuously navigating the pitfalls and politics of everyday existence, stuck in Groundhog Day. People who are going round in circles yet can't seem to make ends meet.

* The people who are genuinely trying their best but forever getting nowhere, who do everything they can to make a difference, but nothing seems to change. For those who are trying to be different, but for whom change seems to take forever. For those who are paralysed by social conformity. For those people who've peaked but don't like the view, or the ones that are continually scrambling around the foothills, never really getting their dreams off the ground. People of every colour, orientation, and persuasion whom, no matter how hard they try, life is even more trying.

* Those people who are past caring but think they probably should.

* Those who desperately need a moral nudge to overcome the selfish inertia of knowing which side their bread is buttered, who have their cake and eat it, who have too much of a good thing.

* Those people who have become disillusioned with a saccharine self-help narrative: struggling with adopting a more 'positive' perspective. For the readers who only ever stumble through the first chapter. For those who have tried endless possibilities but always return to the same conclusion: life is unrelenting and unyielding. Impossible, even. For those who have tried and failed, who are trying and failing.

In short, this is a book for everyone.

This book, however, is especially for **YOU**.

I've spent years traversing highways and byways peddling words, extolling the benefits of becoming the 'best version of yourself'. It's a phrase we hear increasingly often, one that's permeated popular culture. Sometimes, I have to confess, it feels a little hollow. Don't get me wrong, it's an admirable sentiment, and fortunately one I broadly subscribe to (you can't be anyone else, after all).

Increasingly however, there is a slightly jarring narrative in the field of self-help, one that seems to favour pseudo change and internal realignment, rather than the realisation of actual, tangible improvement and meaningful change. To some, wellbeing is seemingly just a matter of angles, perceptions, smoke and mirrors. A 'sleight-of-head' is all that's required.

The problem, we're led to believe, is how things seem. We're merely looking at things the wrong way. This can feel somewhat dismissive, a superficial solution to often deeper-rooted difficulties. At best, we may find fleeting relief, at worst, our troubles become compounded and exacerbated. A sleight-of-head might help us drop off to sleep at night or get out of bed in the morning a little spritelier, but it does nothing for the bits in between. Our lives predominantly consist of the in-between bits, plumping our existence. We need to do more than just think about it.

People, places, circumstance, relationships, events, jobs, money (or the lack of) are invariably the underlying problems, and it's not unsightly negativism to acknowledge this. When you don't have enough food to eat, it's an issue – the grumbling stomach will always overrule the mind. You can't just think you're not hungry. When you're stuck in an unrewarding and unfulfilling job, day-in day-out, the job is part of the problem, not just the way you're looking at it. An abusive relationship cannot be ignored by refocusing. Anxiety, stress and depression are the culmination of tangible, complex challenges. Homelessness is not just a matter of perspective. The real world contains real problems requiring real solutions.

> **When enough is enough, don't just tackle the thinking, address the underlying cause. When you've had enough of putting-up with it, it's time to set-about sorting the 'it'. It's time to move from surviving to thriving. To up your resilience.**

Perhaps you're blissfully happy as you are, quietly contented with your lot and ticking over just fine. Or quite possibly, you're one of those millions of people who, on the face of it, are blissfully happy and quietly contented with your lot, but on the inside are far from it. Very far from it. Whatever it is.

Life can seem an impossible conundrum for many – or maybe even most – of us at some point in our lives. Some acknowledge this and seek solace in the form of religion, therapy, medication, music, drugs, virtuality, sexuality … pretty much anything, in fact, that provides a nullifying distraction from reality. Maybe that helps in the short term, but avoiding life is no way to live one.

A sizeable proportion of the population deals with life's conundrums by not dealing with them. We bury our head in the sand and hope that things will somehow magically improve. We buy in to blissful oblivion. We pretend that we're managing just fine, considering, and everything will be okay. Spiralling credit card bills are just an inevitable by-product of increasingly stretched household finances in tough economic circumstances. Fast-food and take-away convenience meals help sustain us when we don't have sufficient time to prepare healthy food. Busy parents outsource parenting to before-and-after-school clubs. It's just the way it is. Isn't it?

We work harder and longer in jobs that are seemingly harder and all-consuming. In jobs that many of us have quietly grown to loathe and despise, contrary to our true callings. There are good days and bad days, but increasingly – they're mostly bad.

Pretending is a handy mechanism for managing daily life. In the short term, at least. Facing up to things is hard. Today will almost certainly be easier if you continue pretending everything is okay. You will get through it. Probably. You'll probably manage tomorrow, too, and maybe even stumble your way towards the sanctuary of the weekend.

However, zoom in to your future, Google-maps fashion and, on closer inspection, you'll notice a gradual pattern over time. It's best described as an inexorable decline. At worst, we'll call it the beginning of the end. There are millions and millions of people doing just enough to survive another day, in the vain hope that tomorrow will be better, or hopefully not quite as tough as today. Existing, not living. Just getting by until it's time to say goodbye.

Make no mistake, life is genuinely tough. In the wider world it feels like catastrophe is just around the corner. Global pandemics, wars and economic meltdown are very real. Adopting a positive attitude doesn't cut it.

Some psychologists would suggest it's our thinking at fault: an inability to see the bigger picture and focus on a better future. Our experiences are created from the inner machinations of our brain; a little mental tinkering is all that's required. It's not *what* we see, it's the way that we see it…

I'm not saying that attitude isn't important (it is), but too often it remains a bafflingly abstract solution, a nice sufficiently woolly idea to nurture when conditions are conducive. Just like it's easy for the wealthy to extol the value of the simple things in life, positivity grows best in a rosy garden that, quite frankly, we are not all party to. When the weeds are threatening to take over, it's not so straightforward. The vagaries of an upbeat inner world are trumped by crushing real-world hardship every time. The hungry are hungry, the sick are sick, and the poor cannot magically conjure happy pounds and pence. Attitude is important. But it's a starting point situated a long, long way from the solution.

Hardship and suffering are not the exclusive domains of any single socio-economic demographic. Closer to the homes of those who seemingly have it all, peek behind the doors of suburbia and you'll likely witness a multitude of problems. Toothache, vet's bills, noisy neighbours, leaky gutters, dementia, rising damp, closing-down sales, ingrown toenails, outgrown school shoes, marriage, divorce, adoption, separation, cremation, roadworks, fireworks, old age and wheelie bins… Planet Earth can be a real headache.

Things aren't going to suddenly get better on their own

The plain and simple truth is that pain and hardship are not going to magically go away anytime soon. It's not suddenly going to get any better. The chances are, you're not going to win 'big' on the lottery. That dream job, assuming it actually exists, has not got your name on it. You're not even on the shortlist. There's a strong possibility that the sun won't shine today, or the rain will continue to fall. The weather really doesn't give two hoots whether you've just had your hair done especially, or that you didn't think to bring a jumper. Your kids, lovely as they are, have their own problems to contend with. Your spouse is at the centre of their very own all-encompassing universe. You're not the only one with issues.

The world is tough. FACT.

Pretending otherwise might be a convenient (albeit delusional) solution, but it doesn't actually solve anything. Mental health is at an all-time low, because real people have real problems that they feel really bad about in their real everyday miserable lives. Changing 'you' for the better is only half the story. 'Change' might happen on the inside, but it's only sustainable if it manifests on the outside. Change on the inside isn't actually change at all, it's just a trick of the mind. It's just pretending that things are looking up to make us feel a little bit better. Feelings matter, of course, but matter matters more.

It could be argued that the goal of life is to survive it, just long enough to create new life by causing something of a familial stir in between. We're simply passing on the genetic baton. Enter, exist, exit. A dead end. It doesn't get much simpler than that. The aim of the game is to play it for as long as possible.

Whilst life can be undeniably tough at times, the truth of the matter is it's probably a whole lot easier now than it has been through the entirety of human history. It doesn't feel like that, of course, because we've only been around for an evolutionary blink of an eye – for our personal history. We can only compare today with yesterday, in anticipation of tomorrow. Relatively speaking, though, things feel hard.

Survival requires resilience. A lot of it. Resilience is what keeps us all going when the going gets tough. Resilience is the cornerstone of endurance and ensures that we continue to put up with a lot, again and again. We repeatedly put up with our boss because we need to meet the monthly mortgage repayments. Your boss repeatedly puts up with you because she has to meet her monthly mortgage repayments. We put up with our noisy, inconsiderate neighbours because we don't want to move, can't afford to, and why should we anyway? We put up with pain because we don't want to go to the doctors and chance hearing something even more painful. We put up with a lot.

Resilience is what drags us out of bed in the morning kicking and screaming; to do the stuff we have to do, even when we don't want to, again and again and again. Resilience is a sometimes unwelcome voice in your head pushing you to keep going. It keeps you going back for more even when you've had more than enough. Resilience keeps our head above the water when we're not feeling particularly buoyant.

Resilience feeds necessity. It works on a principle of supply-and-demand. It ensures we meet the bottom line – doing just enough to get by, and no more. To live another day. Doing just enough, requires just enough resilience.

No one aims for a surplus of resilience; we 'deal with it' and hurriedly move on to happier times requiring less effort, exertion and stress. It's like a hospital; you don't go there unless it's absolutely necessary. Resilience is employed primarily to endure and is seen as an uncomfortable necessity. It's equated with hardship and battling on through. We draw on it rather than build on it.

We need to upgrade

But what if we could harness resilience to aspire and elevate? What if we could supersize it? What if it could be used as a tool to excel, to deploy at will and exceed expectation rather than falling back upon as a last resort? What if we could supplement our reservoirs of resilience, upping our endeavour to make an authentic positive difference? What if we were able to supercharge our resilience? What if we could learn to be better at being happier and more positive? What if we could learn to be better at being better?

Then we'd have **resilience 2.0**. A tool for growth and improvement, rather than just pain management.

You don't have to look far to witness the value of harnessing positive resilience. Elite sportsmen and women, big business, entrepreneurs, trailblazers, world-leading visionaries and just about anyone who's successful in their field, have crafted, cultivated and nurtured resilience to push boundaries and seize opportunity.

Resilience has been channelled to upgrade people's lives from doing things because they 'have to', to doing things 'better than they have to'. Indeed, because they want to. Upgrading to resilience 2.0 makes a real-world difference, materially changing options, opportunities and shaking-up the status quo. It's not just about thinking positively, but actively making a difference to the habits, circumstances and routines which define and curtail daily lives.

Because crafting resilience is all about getting things done in the real world, there are all sorts of practical things that we can tangibly action rather than becoming over-reliant on changing our mood or our thinking. Sure, feelings and emotions always come into things, but changing behaviour is best achieved by positive proactive deeds. Our feelings and emotions are rarely isolated from the practicalities of our immediate surroundings. In some quarters there's an expectation that wellbeing is about being 'happy with our lot'. All that's required is an attitude of gratitude. It doesn't work.

Being happy with your 'lot' is a lot easier if your lot is something that you are aligned with: something that floats your boat and contributes to a sense of purpose. That doesn't mean that maintaining perspective is not important, just that taking actual steps to create change is more meaningful than merely thinking about it. Mindful gymnastics alone can be unhelpful and even damaging. They deny and obscure the root causes of dissatisfaction, muddying the waters of mental health rather than addressing the underlying issues. The ability to look at scenarios from different angles is a valuable tool, of course, just so long as it doesn't stop at the looking.

Real change requires real action. Fortunately, change is something that can be learnt. Indeed, 'change' and learning are synonymous. Change of mind, action or process requires learning alternative reason, rationale, knowledge or skills.

To learn something new, we must change our existing model of the world. You can't learn without facilitating change, you can't change without learning something new.

Change = learning

Learning = change

The two aren't always proportional (you may have to learn a lot to make a little change or vice-versa) but they are inextricably linked.

For our purposes, resilience is key to harnessing the relationship between learning and change for the better. It's the practical application driving the equation: the sum total of the key constituent parts. Underpinning resilience, is an understanding of the magnitude of change, and how to successfully navigate it.

Chapter 2

The Change Equation

Change is both essential and inevitable. Nothing stays the same. This isn't news – we all know this, yet can be woefully ill-prepared for it, and sometimes even stubbornly resistant. Far from embracing change, we often actively avoid it. We don't think we're avoiding it. We pretend we're moving with the times with varying degrees of belligerence; it's just that the times are moving at light speed. So fast, in fact, that relatively speaking, we're practically in reverse gear. We're moonwalking our way through evolutionary relativity.

The world is changing fast – we need to change too

Just to put this into some sort of perspective, we'll step back into the swinging 1960s. Black and white TV, Beatlemania, the miniskirt and Gordon Moore.

Gordon was big into chips. Not the salt-and-vinegar variety, but the sort that give computers their technological oomph and processing power. As a co-founder of the computer giant INTEL, Gordon knew a thing or two. Of particular note was his astute observation that the number of transistors a microchip could accommodate was rapidly increasing, due to advancements in technology, manufacturing, engineering, computing and science. Roughly speaking, they were doubling every two years, increasing exponentially. The rate they were increasing at was faster than the increase. Bear with me.

More transistors meant faster, more powerful microchips, and greater computer processing power. Gordon's observation became known as 'Moore's Law' and has been used as a broad estimation of the rate of technological growth ever since. There's some debate about the precise pace of change, but the consensus is that it's pretty rapid. Some predictions suggest that over the next 100 years (judging by the current rate of progress) we can expect to experience a whopping 20,000 years' worth of change. That's more change in one lifetime than from when Woolly Mammoths were rocking the Ice Age to now!

We'll start a new paragraph whilst that sinks in.

Whether or not that will hold true remains to be seen, but we shouldn't be surprised by the startling magnitude of such a prediction, considering how the digital age has exploded and revolutionised life over the last 20 years. Whatever the next hundred years has in store will likely be a far cry from the current way of things. The clues are all around us, too. We've got a whole load of space-age stuff going on in our homes, workplaces, and the commute in between, and the space-age stuff has got decidedly even more space-age. Artificial intelligence just got real.

Such is the rate and rapidity of change, that it's no longer the demands of the future we're grappling with. The future is already here. Anyone trying to live a pre-2019 existence will no-doubt be struggling to work, bank, shop, medicate, navigate, communicate, travel… live. We've all got to move with the times – like it or not – which means countering umpteen millennia's worth of ingrained evolutionary psychology and circuitry.

Being human hasn't just happened overnight. Neither has it just happened, it's a result of forever's worth of Darwinian tweaking. As an indicator of why we're such stuck-in-the-muds, we need to go back to times when we were hunter-gathers, spending most of our time, err… hunting and gathering, and trying not to get stuck in the mud.

Human beings have never been the fastest mammal, but we are one of the coolest. Literally, that is, not figuratively. Historically, supper entailed pursuing a gazelle over the plains of the Serengeti for mile after mile after mile. We weren't quick enough or quiet enough to get into spearing range, but we didn't need to be. The main course might have been more fleet of foot, but it also generated a lot of heat very quickly, thus only managing short bursts of speed before needing to stop and cool down. All our pedestrian ancestors had to do, was keep the labouring gazelle in sight, ushering it on when it required a rest, until it eventually keeled over with exhaustion. Hence, we never really pushed the pursuit, we did just enough for just long enough. We mastered the art of sitting it out.

But there's also another consideration. The hunter also kept a self-preservatory eye open just in case a no-nonsense predator higher up the food chain decided to put in an appearance. Being mindful of a hungry lion's ability to put a stone-age spanner in the works, early man kept a little energy back in reserve, in case some sort of emergency evasive action was needed. Hence, we have evolved with bodies built for performance, but brains programmed for efficiency. We're Ferraris perennially cruising in second gear. We're in cruise control, albeit with questionable levels of control. We are not really sure how to handle our potential.

Efficiency equates to routine, going about our daily business on autopilot utilising as little effort as possible. You might not think you do, but you do (or rather you don't). The 'not thinking' part is actually a prime example of our efficiency mindset. We are creatures of habit – even those of us who consider ourselves not to be. If you consider yourself not to be, you are a creature of 'considering yourself not to be,' which is a habit in itself…

Your whole life might be one great big habit – and not necessarily a good one, or at least one that does you justice. From the moment we wake in the morning and reach for our phones, the habitual cycle kicks in. We choose the same breakfast cereal, and endeavour to source our favourite bowl and spoon. Our bathroom routine deviates very little, as we reach bleary-eyed for the basic utilities and commodities that we hope will make us presentable. Obviously, you put on your underwear before your socks, because the other way around would be just plain wrong. We travel to work by the same routes, on the same buses and trains, listening to the same old news, on the same radio stations and podcasts, before ending up in the same place all over again. We park in the bay where we always park, on tarmac, in life. Routinely navigating the world is easier in the immediacy because we don't have to think about it. We get by without the conscious mental contortions required by grappling with difference.

We get by, but little more. Perhaps even begrudgingly. Although we retort 'mustn't grumble' we can't resist doing exactly that. Real grumbling and virtual grumbling. But it is possible to change, if we so choose. We can learn to change and change how we learn.

> **We can learn to be better if we get better at learning. We can learn resilience.**

But there's something to consider first: the blame game.

Chapter 3

The Blame Game

Just take a moment to consider the flip side of the coin. Think about the consequences of resisting change, of remaining inflexible in a changing world. If you put aside the fact that it's ultimately futile and unavoidable, it can prove damaging and destructive. Change avoidance creates a toxic environment that not only has a detrimental effect on you, but negatively impacts upon the people around you. This is the case in both our personal and professional lives, individually and collectively.

The Canadian psychologist, Ben Dattner*, masterfully describes the cycle of deterioration arising from sticking our heads in the sand for far too long. Avoiding change doesn't actually avoid it, just kicks the can further down the line. In doing so it compounds the issue, creating a concertina effect, exacerbating and entrenching issues and difficulties. Avoidance creates jagged edges. If change isn't addressed in a timely fashion it takes us to a point from which there is no return. A bad situation can no longer be salvaged, going from bad to much, much worse. Irretrievably worse.

Sometimes change comes out of the blue and surprises us, but more often than not it creeps up on us more subtly. We become increasingly aware over a period of time that something's got to give, with rising levels of stress and anxiety bubbling to the surface. We just about manage from day to day, managing a little less each day, avoiding the underlying issues, until things come to a head and we lose our head. Usually later rather than sooner, and in a rather protracted and painful way.

*Founder of Dattner Consulting (www.dattnerconsulting.com)

It eventually becomes plainly obvious that survival depends on taking evasive action. We are faced with a stark choice between doing something – anything – or suffering the catastrophic consequences of inaction. Faced with such a choice, we have to act, regardless of how painful it is. Not acting is too nuclear to contemplate.

Dattner describes the phases as follows:
* Enthusiasm
* Disillusionment
* Panic
* Search for the guilty
* Punishment of the innocent
* Rewards for the uninvolved.

Dattner related this cycle to the workplace, but it's just as commonplace in our personal lives as our working lives. My wife, Helen, reminded me of a family wedding we were scheduled to attend.

Enthusiasm
The 'big day' was fast approaching. We were all looking forward to a 'bit of a do'. Outfits were sorted, including one that would require Helen (in her opinion) to lose a few pounds. Fortunately, a particular diet had been recommended by a friend, guaranteeing just that. Sorted.

Disillusionment
Unfortunately, after two weeks of pursuing the so-called 'miracle diet' there had been no miracle.

Panic
The big day was fast approaching. The dress had already been purchased. Time was running out. The tension was palpable.

Search for the guilty

Evidently, Helen had not yet achieved her optimal dress size because of years spent selflessly doting upon the rest of the family. We were to blame.

Punishment of the innocent.

All biscuits, crisps, snacks and sugary treats were subsequently banned. The whole family had to survive solely on lettuce leaves and celery.

Rewards for the uninvolved

A well-known multi-million-pound clothes retailer profited from the purchase of a brand-new alternative dress.

Change is best addressed sooner rather than later

It's a bit like visiting the dentist. No one really looks forward to visiting the dentist (perhaps with the exception of the dentist) and it's the same with the prospect of change. We try to put it off. When we eventually relent, the whole experience feels somewhat out of our control. It's also accompanied by a degree of discomfort, and we don't know how long the whole procedure will take. Both dentistry and change also require significant amounts of investment. We have cause to wonder if it's really worth it. Avoiding your regular check-up, however, only tends to make matters worse and exacerbates any underlying problems. It's the same with change. Toothaches lead to rotten teeth. Change-ache erodes the enamel of life.

Despite being inevitable, and perhaps even because of it, change can feel frightening and daunting. Change requires deviation from our comfortable norms and parameters and venturing into a landscape of unknowns and uncertainty. It's investment-heavy, requiring us to accommodate new practices, processes and meaning, obliging us to rethink our view of both the world and ourselves, adjusting and acting in accordance.

But maybe change-in-itself, isn't scary. We don't mind changing our underwear, after all. The weather can change from hour to hour, but most of us take it in our stride. People come and go, personally and professionally and, for the most part, it's business as usual after some degree of recalibration. We manage. We take small change in our stride.

It's the magnitude of change that we struggle with

Big change is often viewed as a destabilising influence to be avoided. It might not actually be destabilising, but the surrounding narrative doesn't do us any favours. We think in terms of black and white. You know what you're good at and avoid what you're not. The rudiments of life are quickly categorised as easy or hard. We avoid the hard, not necessarily because it is hard, but because we don't like the thought that it might be, and we might be found lacking. Instead of speaking from experience, our limiting projections substitute the lack of it.

That's not to say that change isn't a challenge, just that we subconsciously don't bother to find out, because we've already made our minds up. 'Don't ask me how I know, I just do…' Only we don't. We're good at making uninformed, ill-informed third-person decisions. Or maybe you've suffered some sort of unfortunate setback in the past and have generalised ever since. You don't want to risk going there again, so you end up not really going anywhere.

We often make up our mind about the merits of something very quickly rather than making an educated decision. We jump to a conclusion without expending too much time and energy over it. The conclusions are usually the comfortable ones that sit cosily within our pre-conceived existing notions of the world, the ones that endorse our current modus operandi. The ones that aren't too much of a leap. Change is not black or white, however. It is absolutely not polarised, but sits on a gradual, graded sliding scale that is constantly shifting and evolving for every single one of us.

> **True change helps us evolve from ignorance to excellence.**

Whilst it's a continuum, there are a few useful benchmarks to help navigate between the deep end and the shallow end. These benchmarks aren't new, but they might be new to you. It seems that we learn all sorts at school, apart from how to actually *learn*. This would be a good place to start.

As I mentioned earlier: if you want to learn to be better, you've got to first become better at learning.

The concrete steps traversed when learning to change act like stepping stones. They bridge the gap between the known and the unknown and effectively make the process more manageable and approachable. Knowing what each stage looks and feels like is key to understanding the magnitude of challenge; you become informed and enlightened regarding what needs to be 'done'. Without comprehension of the true scale of change, we're reluctant to fully engage and/or woefully unprepared.

Channelling change into meaningful transformation requires something extra, however. Understanding the magnitude of change is one thing, knowing what to do about it – and how to set about it – is another thing entirely. Only by changing both perspective and behaviour can you make a genuine positive lasting difference.

All growth, development and improvement necessitate the navigation of distinct stages. As discussed, we have a predisposition for doing just enough to get by in many aspects of our lives, illustrating our brains' efficiency in the short term. You'll notice that there are some skills that you've absolutely nailed, whilst remaining distinctly lacklustre at others.

'Lacklustre' equates to doing enough to get by. It's the baseline for survival and we typically do just that, and not a whole lot more. We're effort minimalists. Appreciating the true scale of change we're faced with helps us to maximise our potential, or at least be not quite so minimal.

Remaining oblivious to the true extent of a task or challenge means we're beaten almost before we start. It's a huge step into the unknown. Not knowing what you're getting yourself in to creates unease and uncertainty that undermines our conviction and application. With little concept of the potential timescales involved, we become disillusioned very quickly. Many people who take up playing a musical instrument, for instance, anticipate being much better than they actually become, and a whole lot sooner! The discrepancy between expectation and reality causes us to become frustrated and throw in the towel. Learning to play the guitar becomes a temporary (and maybe even expensive) short-lived fad. This is not so much to do with any lack of musical ability, rather an inability to cope with the discrepancy.

We're great at starting and rubbish at finishing. Whether it's penning that book you've always wanted to write, training for a half-marathon, starting your own business… we're woefully unprepared for the magnitude of the task. We fail not because of our ability, but of the unknown quantity before us, and the mismanagement of that unknown.

Chapter 4

The Increments of Improvement

Understanding the distinctly different stages of change* helps us to appreciate the time and effort involved. It's also a starting point for considering the underlying driving behaviours.

Unconscious incompetence – having no idea

The baseline of change is being blissfully unaware of the need to change. These are the things that you don't know that you don't know. Blissful ignorance has not yet alerted you to the existence of certain facets of knowledge, skill, practice or expertise that inhabit the universal ether. In short, you are in the dark and you're not aware you're in the dark.

Conscious incompetence – ah! I know what you mean...

Conscious incompetence is a moment of realisation: the sound of the penny dropping. You become manifestly aware of a concept, practice, theory or behaviour that has, until now, safely bypassed you. That's not to say you were better off, just that until this point you didn't know that you were better off – or not – because that point of reference didn't exist. Conscious incompetence is the moment that Pandora's Box is opened: there's no going back. You can't become unaware of the existence of... er... existence. There's no way of 'unseeing it' even if you don't really understand what 'it' is.

Becoming consciously incompetent is on some level a call to action, even if it's not necessarily through choice. Awareness of something means we have to process it in some way, whether that be discarding it, acknowledging it or filing it for later. It's impossible not to register on some level. There is no going back.

*The four stages of competence first appeared in *Management of Training Programs* (1960) F A DePhillips, W M Berliner, J J Cribbin. Published by Richard D Irwin, Inc.

Conscious incompetence means things play on your mind. You sense something could or should be addressed but are aware you don't have the skills, know-how or inclination to deal with it.

Conscious incompetence could be:

There are all sorts of means by which we deal with being consciously incompetent – or not. Not dealing, is very common, because of a reluctance to expend significant time, effort or headspace. We dismiss the importance of that which we know little about, thus excusing ourselves from finding out more. We don't like to admit our ignorance or our limitations, especially to ourselves. Admitting we don't know how to do something can feel an afront to our self-esteem. We ignore our ignorance.

It's common to hark back to a time when we remained blissfully in the dark. For some, it's a coping strategy. The amount of people who become acutely aware that they are eating too much, drinking too much and compromising their health by a toxic lifestyle, yet continue to compromise is staggering. Despite, on some level, most of us knowing about the damage we are doing to ourselves (or our families),

Resilience 2.0: Embracing Challenge and Change

we choose to ignore it. We actively choose not to change, even when we are aware of the seriousness of the potential consequences.

The truth? You can try to avoid change but it won't avoid you.

Change is non-negotiable. It can be opposed to some extent, perhaps even stalled, but ultimately resistance is futile; time moves on. But whilst change is inevitable, that doesn't mean that we can't shape it, harness it and sculpt it. Rather than avoiding it, it's possible to embrace it. We can all change for the better.

Conscious competence – off with the stabilisers

The third stage of dealing with change is a tough one. It feels like hard work because it is. It's the moment when we've pulled our head out of the sand and confronted the need to evolve, to do something and take action. Initially, this stage can feel like a prolonged failure. Whilst there's some variation in how well we 'take' to acquiring a new skill, the majority of us are not like the proverbial 'duck to water'. In bike parlance, the stabilisers have been removed and things feel very wobbly.

A skill is 'new' because we have no (or very limited) direct experience of it. Thus far, we have dabbled and not yet acquired any degree of competency. Acquisition is therefore a rumbustious process of trial and error. The errors are a rich source of feedback.

Conscious competence requires a great deal of focus and effort whilst we grapple with the intricacies of a brave new world. Our conscious brain prompts us to gauge the varying degrees of success when trialling different approaches, desperately searching for something that might contribute to a blueprint of understanding. All this endeavour requires a great deal of perspiration and no little inspiration, as we constantly seek new and alternative angles of approaching the task in question.

After a certain amount of time, most of us (if the skill is not too complex) achieve some modicum of success, whilst experiencing our fair share of failure, too. We've expended significant effort to achieve even moderate results or sporadic wins. This modest degree of change is all that many of us ever realise, yet often we deem it sufficient to make an informed judgement. Cue generalisations: 'We've given it a go… our best shot… it's not for me…' We look for a get-out clause, because it really doesn't feel like it's worth all the effort.

Arguably, you've applied yourself to the task in hand and found it to be hard work. Because hard work feels like hard work, we tend to alleviate the discomfort at the earliest possible opportunity, particularly if the payback seems limited. Having dallied with something new, we can sanctimoniously dismiss it through first-hand experience.

Many people consider themselves sufficiently qualified to make sweeping judgements when consciously competent. We possess some general exposure but insufficient grasp of the intricacies or specifics.

Conscious competence could be:

A yEll0w ℬeLt 1n kAratE
Grade 1 In piaNo
1 mOnth's gym mɑmBershlp
AcHiEVinG stUd3Nt tɑcker ST@tUs
R3cEív1nG seCond-haNd neWs
r3adiNg the first 3 chapters
tUnNing Y0uR f1rSt 5K
sEtt1ng the wɑshing machiNe tiMer
a first fl1Ght abr0ad
f0rMinG A tHird-haNd perSpEctive

Unconscious competence – the alchemy of change

Change has felt like hard work up until now. Unconscious competence is the point at which change doesn't feel like change any more; we have absorbed new learnings and broadened our existing repertoire of skills. We've succeeded at learning something 'new' when it no longer feels 'new' anymore – or indeed like 'learning'. It becomes part of us and who we are.

The knowledge, skills and abilities that we come to take for granted inhabit the cognitive domain of low-maintenance auto-functionality. Remember the terror experienced in your first few driving lessons? Many of us struggled with the dexterity of operating three pedals with only two feet. Chances are if you've been driving a few years, you no longer give it a second thought. Funny that. We can navigate our way to work with ease whilst anticipating the forthcoming day. It's difficult to recall whether we were stopped at traffic lights, such is the minimal conscious attention now required. What was once all-consuming is now an afterthought or requires little thought at all.

Unconscious competence is the first time that real value can be added; the benefits gained finally outweigh the expenditure of time and effort. Up until now, there has been significant investment with little return.

Using the analogy of learning to ride a bike, thus far staying upright has been all-encompassing. Unconscious competence signals achieving the minimum level of skill required to cycle to the shops, tackle some gentle mountain biking or safely complete a lap around the local BMX track. Unconscious competence is an entry level requirement. Up until this point, there is no practical benefit from your level of development. The preceding stage, conscious competence, only weans you off the stabilisers.

In all stages prior to this, the application required takes more out of you than any perceived beneficial return. Up until this point, endeavour has been absorbed as unrealised potential, often hidden to such an extent we can feel somewhat despondent, bemoaning our efforts have been in vain. Many of us simply never reach the heady heights of unconscious competence, not realising just how close we may have come. We give up too soon.

Change is taking place below the surface, however, just not realised. We don't see or feel our progress, just like we cannot witness ourselves grow, or grow old. The increments are not readily distinguishable from minute to minute, day to day, or from week to week. Outwardly, you still can't 'do' whatever it is you set out to achieve, but you have become better at failing. Success is refined failure. When failure becomes ultra-refined a change in state occurs, namely success. Once all the 'wrong' adjustments have been exhausted, the feedback culminates in progress.

The foibles of evolution make our perceived shortfalls glaringly obvious and constantly serve to remind us of our limitations. The stuff we can't do is seemingly more of a problem than the stuff we can, therefore we fixate on the negative.

Go back far enough, and you start to see how our thinking has evolved.

Broadly speaking, in historical terms, the further back you go the tougher life was. Danger and jeopardy lurked everywhere, of which we soon learned the hard way to be mindful of. Wild animals, warring factions, a scarcity of food, exposure, disease, infection; staying alive was an all-encompassing struggle. The consequences of carelessness in such a hostile environment were not just unforgiving – they were fatal. Our evolutionary existence has required us to become proficient at registering potential mishap, misadventure and disaster. As a species, we've become good at spotting the bad. Not just clear and present danger, but potential risks. We construct threats, mentally rehearsing our self-preservation strategy, just in case.

Hence our perceptual bandwidth has evolved to be largely negatively orientated, leaving little room for registering small victories. We have grown tone deaf to our improvements, and then remarkably quick to delete them. We reframe our new skills as ones that have always existed and have scant regard for self-congratulatory inner small talk.

Unconscious competence could be:

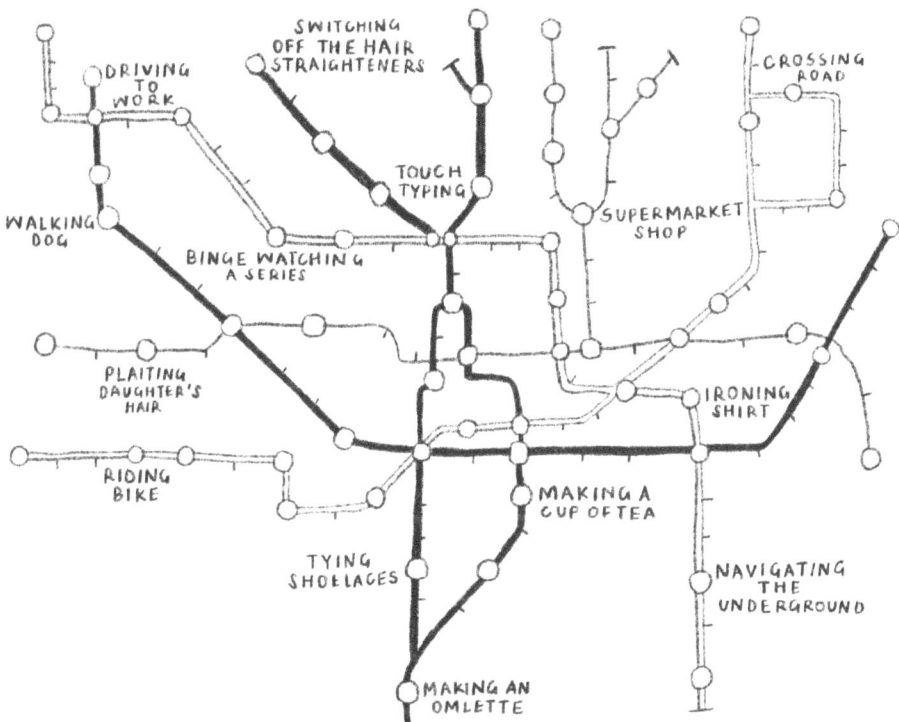

Mastery – voila!

Whilst functionality is obtained with unconscious competence, the real fun lies within mastering a particular challenge, change or skill. Mastery is the point at which a skill becomes an ingrained talent to be enjoyed, applied, exercised and elaborated upon (although, there's always room for improvement!). Your brain has learnt to hardwire a complex set of neural connections, enabling the requisite electrical signals to flash effortlessly (or at least unconsciously) around the highways and byways of your nervous system. Your brain works faster without you interfering; mastery is an automatic fast-tracked response – a superpower. You can do it expertly without thinking. In fact, if you try thinking – commonly known as 'overthinking' – you tend to fall apart.

Stuff you've mastered can almost be done blindfolded.

Mastery is when everyone – including yourself – sits up and takes notice. It is the culmination of the ability, drive and desire to do something better than you have to. Indeed, because you want to. Learning to refine and improve your technique and repertoire subsequently unlocks more complex and difficult possibilities. The extent to which a skill can be mastered is a measure of not just your potential but (perhaps more importantly) the inclination to explore it. You set your own ceilings.

We can normally get by just fine without the need to master the world. Just doing enough is not a result of mastery. Mastery is only achieved when we are personally invested. It requires additional effort and endeavour, because a working level of competence has already been achieved. We can get by in most situations without mastery. We have to 'want' to develop further to fulfil some sort of intrinsically or extrinsically motivated desire. Intrinsic motivation primarily satisfies yourself, extrinsic motivation references others. Mastery requires drive, which is predominantly an inside job.

The pace of improvement usually slows in search of mastery, as the number of 'quick gains' have, by now, significantly diminished. This can affect our drive to continually pursue change and improvement, because the amount of effort required increases for proportionally dwindling returns.

Mastery could be:

The business of change

The truth is, if you're not in the business of change, you're in the wrong business. Individuals, businesses and organisations that don't adapt, don't end up doing very much. The extent to which a business embraces each developmental stage is a strong indicator of its longevity. Apportioning resources to each area is the best way of futureproofing.

We'll consider the stages out of 'order' to illustrate their organisational value for a business.

Unconscious competence (consolidation)	These are the things your business does automatically; the day-to-day running and administration of processes, goods, services and dealings with customers and commerce. These are the nuts and bolts of doing what's required to function effectively and efficiently. Processes work and are relatively smooth and streamlined. Things get done. The business of business is second nature, everyone is aware of their role

	and has the necessary skills, expertise, tools and understanding to fulfil their individual and collective remit. Without achieving unconscious competence in all departments, a business will not be sustainable. In truth, work doesn't work very well until you reach unconscious competence. Unconscious competence is essential for **consolidation**.
Mastery (innovation)	Mastery is the level of competence that makes you stand out from the crowd. Essentially, you are providing a better service than your competitors, over-delivering and exceeding customer expectations. This is the art of doing things 'better than you have to.' Mastery will bolster your name and reputation and help grow your client base, making you about more than just the 'bottom line'. You might not be the cheapest provider out there, but you're evidently worth it. Delivering at a level of mastery increases customer loyalty. As leaders in your field, mastery underlines your ability to **innovate**.
Conscience incompetence (initiation)	This stage of development reflects honest recognition of the things that you are currently not doing. This is the stuff that might be on the peripheries of your radar but have conveniently stayed there, safely out of the way. The things that have not yet made it on to your list of priorities or been formally recognised in any way. Your competitors may or may not be considering them, and they may or may not be benefitting from them (yet). Although some of them likely will be. Your operations, systems and profit margins are probably healthy, which means that

	entertaining thoughts about 'fixing things that aren't broken' feels a little bit counter intuitive. The status quo won't last indefinitely however, so investing in the stuff you don't currently cater for, but others do, will help you to stay competitive. Conscious incompetence is recognition of the willingness to **initiate** development.
Conscious competence (accommodation)	Conscious competence is a stage of adaptation. You are likely investing in recently identified new systems, methods and products that are not paying off. There is likely a disconnect between the input and output, and the seemingly excessive efforts expended into such – as yet – unyielding avenues, can be a source of exasperation and dissonance. You were doing just fine before, after all. Conscious competence can best be described as growing pains. It is an unavoidable intermediary stage, but can be navigated more quickly and painlessly if everyone is pulling in the same direction, rather than resisting. Conscious competence is adopting practical measures to **accommodate** development and improvement.
Unconscious incompetence (speculation)	This is the proverbial golden goose, arguably more valuable than mastery. Identifying investment opportunities that no one else has yet cottoned-on to is a sure-fire way of getting ahead of the game, particularly if you're the only one in that game. By definition, unconscious incompetence suggests unawareness of existence. In an effort to unravel this conundrum, it pays to have working parties actively looking

for the next big thing, rather than just waiting to play catch-up. Waiting to play catch-up means you stand little chance of getting ahead. Identifying the next area for growth and development isn't an exact science, but there is an art to it. Immersing yourself in the conversation is sometimes all that's required to stumble upon the right questions or even the answers. Unconscious incompetence is the cue to speculate upon progress and development. Innovation requires a certain amount of **speculation**.

The process of change is cyclical

Growth – achieving positive results by knowing what to do and doing more of it – is therefore cyclical, requiring sustained effort to continue evolving and developing. It's the ability to keep on 'keeping on' and deal with the magnitude of change rather than feeling hopelessly overwhelmed.

> **The bad news is that the cyclical process of change means that it is never ending.**
>
> **The good news is that the cyclical process of change means that it is never ending.**

Whilst the challenge of evolving is ever-present, so too is our capacity to evolve. With every new situation, predicament or requirement that presents, there is potential to exploit. A problem is merely a challenge we've hitherto failed to meet. The potential for growth is ever-present. Failing to grasp the true scale of change often means we give up before we start. Understanding exactly what the different distinct stages look like helps them to become more tangible, manageable and therefore less daunting. It helps us to process the scale of the challenges we are faced with and comprehend how to go about meeting them.

Knowing what to do sounds obvious when embarking upon a voyage of discovery or journey of improvement, but it is often neglected from the aspiration equation. We often do things purely on the spur of the moment, because it sounded like a good idea at the time or maybe because we were at a loose end. The destination was appealing yet we knew little of the journey involved.

There's a multi-billion-pound industry geared towards planting the seeds of good ideas, selling the seeds of good ideas, without sharing the 'honest' truth about what it takes to cultivate them. This gap is ruthlessly exploited by advertising agencies and marketeers who know we seldom finish what we start. The gap is big business. There are considerably more projects started than finished. A sizeable proportion of people who sign up for a gym membership don't go to the gym. The majority of people who start writing a book will never finish it. There are thousands of pairs of nearly-new running shoes lying dormant in cupboards under the stairs. We've all made snap purchases essential to our brand-new ventures that become redundant all too soon. Lack of completion creates a yearning for achievement, and so the cycle continues. We're on the lookout for the next 'big thing'.

Knowing what to do helps us get by and gives us a fighting chance of scraping through. We're surviving, but we're not thriving. We know what's required, we're trying our best, but that's not enough. And there's nothing more disheartening than feeling like your best efforts are falling short.

Because of evolutionary insecurities, we tend to settle for mediocrity rather than risk greatness. Good enough is good enough, after all.

Resilience is often viewed purely in terms of enduring through thick and thin. Of sticking at it. Of putting up with our lot. As a species, we've had to endure a lot over the years, and have become pretty adept at it. We've learnt the hard way. Entry-level resilience has got its merits; we're still here, after all. We live to fight another day. But it's also got its drawbacks. We get by, but we don't fly.

Life can feel exhausting as we seemingly lurch from one global crisis to another. The majority of us are working harder and longer, often with an air of resignation. We're unfulfilled, on paths that are not of our choosing, leading a merry dance without the merriment. Life seems underwhelming. It certainly doesn't feel very lively. Life expectancy is increasing (with the occasional blip) but we're not acquiring any more value.

Entry level resilience could be:

Destination	Plat	Expected
Ploughing on		Cancelled
A delayed commute		Cancelled
Scraping by		Cancelled
Managing disappointment		Cancelled
SMART targets		Cancelled
Noisy neighbours		Cancelled
Not knowing overdraft		Cancelled
Being treated like a child		Cancelled
Getting older		Cancelled

Departures

Entry-level resilience doesn't cut it, anymore. Something extra is needed to ignite genuine change and make a positive difference. To rise above. To aim higher. To smash it.

What's required, is resilience 2.0.

Resilience 2.0: Embracing Challenge and Change

Chapter 5

Resilience 2.0

Upgrading to resilience 2.0 is about aspiration and reorientation, a seismic shift in attitude, approach and application. It's about small wins and big wins. Galvanised resilience is the ability to activate real change in behaviour to transform results: from surviving the mundane to thriving in the extraordinary. It's about learning to be better. Resilience is about learning to think and behave in certain ways that, when taken together, positively influence outcomes to shatter whatever limitations we have contrived. The sum of resilient behaviours is most definitely greater than the constituent parts.

Knowing what to do is one thing, knowing how to be is quite another. Learning to be transformatively resilient is key to executing real and lasting positive change.

Take a moment to think about your life. I'm guessing you've fit a lot in. I'm also guessing there's been peaks and troughs, highlights and lowlights, ups and downs. All of us have made good and bad decisions. Some of the good decisions may have ultimately proven to be bad. Some of the good decisions may have been genuinely good decisions, but ultimately ineffectual because they were not followed through correctly. It's not always a poor decision which creates the wrong outcome, but our reaction to it. An order is only as good as its execution.

Pursuance of the things that might make a difference is usually curtailed prematurely. We give up and give in when we should instead knuckle down. To progress further than scrabbling conscious competence, we must cultivate the resilience to see the next steps more clearly and through to a positive conclusion. If you want to see things in a better light you've got to bring the torch. You are the illuminating factor: the spark. You, and you alone, can provide it.

Some of these behaviours will be familiar to you, some won't. The minority of people who invest in developing all the behaviours, who collect the full set, are the ones who tend to achieve success rather than just dream about it.

This is a different approach to that taken in many self-help books, in that we're not talking about focusing upon an 'end result'. It's more about the processes required. If we can learn to programme our lives correctly, the outcome should take care of itself. We're interested in best working rather than best work. We are interested in the future, but more interested in the now.

The beauty of fostering resilience by cultivating input, is that the skills, behaviours and attitudes developed are endlessly transferable. Resilience is the solar-powered equivalent of self-help. Focusing on outcomes alone is not quite so sustainable; completing a marathon may help in terms of fitness, for instance, but does little to help with next week's appraisal.

Bolstering resilience focuses upon developing the character underpinning the behaviours. As such, you're investing in the 'person' rather than the end product. When 'you' as an individual are fully functional, you'll be amazed at how other aspects of life, both personal and professional, begin to flourish. True resilience initiates transformative behaviours with diverse applications. It's an example of what you can achieve when you commit wholeheartedly to holistic improvement, rather than dabble. It's the manifestation of everything that makes a positive difference to life on the outside, not just viewed from the inside. Authentic resilience involves more than just thoughts or even words, it's a system of transformative action. It really is possible to turn life around and make good things happen; even 'the sorts of things that don't happen to people like me!'.

Supersizing resilience is key to upping our game. Like any game, there are rules. You don't have to follow them, of course, but playing by the rules will do two things: help you to stay in the game (you've got to be in it to win it, after all) and get the right result.

We'll explore just how to make the rules work for you throughout the remainder of this book, but for now, it's worth becoming familiar with them.

The five essential rules for harnessing resilience involve:

1. **Receptivity**. You've got be up for it.
2. **Risk**. Be prepared to brave it.
3. **Retention**. Stick at it.
4. **Responsibility**. Take accountability for it.
5. **Redefine**. Review your role in it.

Starting with an overview of the 'it' would probably be a good place to start, before we get into the nitty-gritty. The 'it' is a considerable upgrade.

> **To begin with, it's about changing the narrative.**

Chapter 6

The Narrative

> **I'm not sure which is worse: the humdrum lives that many people live or the fact that they've come to accept them.**

I'm not blaming anyone for the predicament they find themselves in. We've already talked about how tough life can be, often through no fault of those individuals at the toughest, sharpest end. Rather, it's an observation of our self-limiting propensity despite huge untapped potential. Or perhaps how we've learnt to be limited by our surroundings, our circumstances, our nearest and dearest or ourselves. We're incredibly quick to adopt a self-defeating narrative that drowns out any chance of a better alternative. The negative self-talk is ridiculously easy to acquire yet devilishly hard to shift.

Examples of negative self-talk:

Resilience 2.0: Embracing Challenge and Change

Changing the narrative is essential for a successful upgrade. To do this, it pays to consider your current programming.

Confirmation bias

Thinking back to your school days, there were particular subjects that you were good or bad at, favoured or otherwise. We quickly decided whether we preferred maths or writing, physical education or art, for instance. I'm not suggesting we don't have have an inherent aptitude for a subject, just that how we come to view that aptitude has a significant bearing upon how we approach it. In short, we like the stuff that we're good at and dislike the stuff we suck at. We play to our strengths and circumnavigate our weaknesses, meaning the strengths receive substantially greater investment. We put our strengths on a pedestal and regularly attend to them. In comparison, our weaknesses are neglected. The disparity becomes more and more pronounced the older we get.

> **Our strengths are the easy option, because it's a comfortable place to reside. We can get by doing just enough.**

Consider going to the gym, which explicitly requires us to make an effort, as an example of our capacity to languish within the mediocrity of 'strength'. There are some exercises we tolerate better than others, so we subtly gravitate towards them. Everyone likes doing arm curls, for instance, yet hamstring curls are avoided at any cost. Arguably, the types and intensity of training we might benefit from most are the sorts that we subconsciously avoid. Skipping legs day isn't a good look. We are, literally, playing to our strengths.

Playing to our strengths in this manner can exacerbate weaknesses. Avoidance creates a growing disparity between what we think we can and cannot do. Upping our resilience crafts a rounded holistic approach. Draw on your strengths and create more strengths.

If you are in work, you will see your role defined in a certain way. This doesn't mean it's the same way others see it – which can, of course, sometimes cause conflict. We quickly make up our minds regarding what constitutes our remit, deciding which of the other areas can either be delegated or relegated in priority (or maybe both). We're constantly making up our minds about what we're good at, what's easy and what's worth avoiding.

We make up our minds as soon as we can because protracted deliberation requires effort. Effort is a furrowed brow, the brain aching as it processes all the various possible computations and permutations. It's easier not to think too hard. It's easier not to think at all. We're comfort thinkers; it's easier to rehash old responses and reflections.

We have a small window of opportunity to process information, before making up our minds. Once minds have been made up, we are stubbornly and infuriatingly closed to any re-evaluation. Human beings don't like to admit they're wrong. We prefer to perpetuate a bad decision than admit a mistake, particularly if we've become entrenched in that position. We are closed-minded. We hold that we're right until the bitter end, even when – deep down – we know that not to be the case. We see any admittance of failure – of making a mistake – akin to weakness. Our feelings override our thinking. Pride trumps everything:

✳ Tears beat perspective
✳ Excitement beats reason
✳ Anger beats logic
✳ Sorrow beats forgiveness
✳ Panic beats reflection
✳ An easy win beats diligence
✳ Nerves negate opportunity
✳ Despair beats repair
✳ Feelings beat thinking
✳ Performance beats introspection

* Prejudice beats evidence
* Easy success beats feedback.

With a closed mind, it's impossible to acknowledge the opportunities that might present. A closed mind is attuned to skirt potential problems, bolstering our default propensity towards doing as little as possible. We avoid being 'wrong' at all costs because that would require some sort of remedial action. It would require change. Change is scary.

Closed thinking is not just the domain of a few narrow-minded individuals, it's a trait that everyone of us has and that requires careful ongoing management. The symptoms can be detected in our everyday lives. Most of these symptoms are not significant in isolation, yet can indicate (or influence) something of a trend or persuasion, if taken in context with each other. These are the small 'bug fixes' that will have a noticeable impact upon your daily operating systems.

Closed behaviours result from closed thinking. Our closures need keeping an eye on, so it's worth knowing what to look out for.

Closed behaviours

There are four key closed behaviours, albeit with some overlap:

CB1 Looks at the impact of rigidly defining a role, professing **'it's not my job'.** Artificially limiting your remit is a great way of curtailing potential.

CB2 Explores an inability to consider new possibilities, clinging to the tired old mantra of **'knowing what I like and liking what I know'.** Curiously, these fixed thinkers rarely appear happy with what they know and are familiar with!

CB3 Is a response to the busy lives we all live, and how our **'limited bandwidth'** curtails capacity for growth.

CB4 Encompasses some of the other **'incidentals'** – dare I say excuses – we find to avoid the discomfort associated with challenge and change.

It is worth taking a closer look at each of the closed behaviours:

CB1: It's not my job...

We've all met a jobsworth: someone who professes to know their role inside-out and is not prepared to deviate or compromise under any circumstances. Because no one knows it better. No one does it better. Think jobsworth, think pedant. A jobsworth knows what's what and doesn't care for what's not. They're direct, inflexible, uncompromising, and sometimes right, sometimes wrong.

The truth is, we all have an inner jobsworth. That inflexible part of us: the side to us that has finally taken a stand against perceived injustices, unnecessary burden and burgeoning bureaucracy. Why should we be the only one to put ourselves out? Enough is enough.

We might not publicly say 'no', but at times we think it. Even if we don't 'think', we think it. A jobsworth approaches any work-related discussion from an obliquely defensive standpoint, and for this reason tends to avoid any formal discussions. Just in case conversations become more pointed and direct and trickier to evade. They are worried that they might be backed into an inescapable work-related corner. A jobsworth won't engage but will confront. Their default body language is epitomised by arms firmly crossed.

Jobsworth thinking makes us more insular; our comfort zone shrinks as we retreat further back from the edges. Effectively, we try and isolate ourselves from the possibility of change and ostracise ourselves from the people who we perceive might suggest it. The number of conversations we have with colleagues decreases, as do the number of colleagues we have those conversations with. We become

Resilience 2.0: Embracing Challenge and Change

more withdrawn in fear of being exposed to painful new practices, procedures and policy.

A jobsworth might…

We ring fence our world as it is and repel any perceived intrusion. We draw a line in the sand, grasp a snapshot in time and hold on as if our life depends on it.

CB2: I know what I like… and I like what I know

> If it ain't broke, don't fix it. It's worked this far. If it was good enough for…

I could go on, but you get the picture. We use all manner of phraseology reinforcing the existing status quo to reassure ourselves that nothing needs to change. In essence, doing okay on the face of it, vindicates doing more of the same. It's essentially a closed feedback loop, where we convince ourselves that we're right until the wheels come off and can be reluctant even then. Sometimes the wheels do spectacularly and dramatically fall off, but usually there's more of a subtle, gradual breakdown, until we wake up sat on the kerbside holding a steering wheel, in true Wile E Coyote fashion.

But we're not in a cartoon and it's not funny. From afar it might sound slightly ridiculous, however. We all know those people who visit the same restaurants and always order the same dishes. We know those people because those people are us. We may not actually order the same specific dish every time, but we do have a tried-and-trusted short list. Our lives are a shortlist of self-limiting options curated solely by ourselves. We choose the reassuringly familiar despite a vast array of riches on offer. We shun endless possibilities just in case we stumble upon something untoward. Avoidance, it seems, trumps possibility.

I'm not saying that what has always proven to be good enough isn't, just that all things inevitably change. If you're not prepared to evolve, the 'change' eventually catches up with you. Sooner or later.

I know what I like…

GROUNDHOG DAY						
S	**M**	**T**	**W**	**T**	**F**	**S**
Work tomorrow	Here we go again	Sigh	Humpday	Friday eve	Phew!	Collapse
Work tomorrow	Here we go again	Sigh	Humpday	Friday eve	Phew!	Collapse
Work tomorrow	Here we go again	Sigh	Humpday	Friday eve	Phew!	Collapse
Work tomorrow	Here we go again	Sigh	Humpday	Friday eve	Phew!	Collapse

Resilience 2.0: Embracing Challenge and Change

CB3: Limited Bandwidth

A friend of mine was musing about oranges a little while ago. Apparently, he'd read in a certain well-known upmarket supermarket magazine, about the steep decline of the sales of oranges. You'd think he would have better things to do, but hey. Apparently, we don't have the time to peel them anymore. I raised a mildly incredulous eyebrow at this point, not entirely convinced that this was the case.

Sensing my misgivings, he enquired if I liked an Easy Peeler. Of course, I do. We all do, don't we? And then the penny dropped; there's two reasons we like Easy Peelers. Yes, they're easy, but significantly, they're also quick and easy. So maybe that particular upmarket supermarket has a point. Busyness is real, and none of us is immune to it.

The problem with busyness is that it preoccupies us with the immediacy of the most pressing demands of the day. Call it prioritising, firefighting, call it what you will, in a world that's full-on we have a considerable amount on our plates. There's a lot of plates spinning. We don't have the bandwidth to accommodate our existing load, let alone anything new. You can probably relate to that feeling of 'having had it up to here'. By 'it', substitute work, health, family life, the cost of living, the daily commute: all manner and number of strains and demands on our time.

We do whatever we need to survive the day because that's about all we can manage. This works to some extent in the short term but is a questionable strategy over the longer term. We have to invest in our futures and the best time to do that is before the future's arrived. Otherwise, we find ourselves woefully unprepared.

> **Unfortunately, an increasingly occupied bandwidth means that what can be put off until tomorrow, usually is.**

When you have limited bandwidth, you…

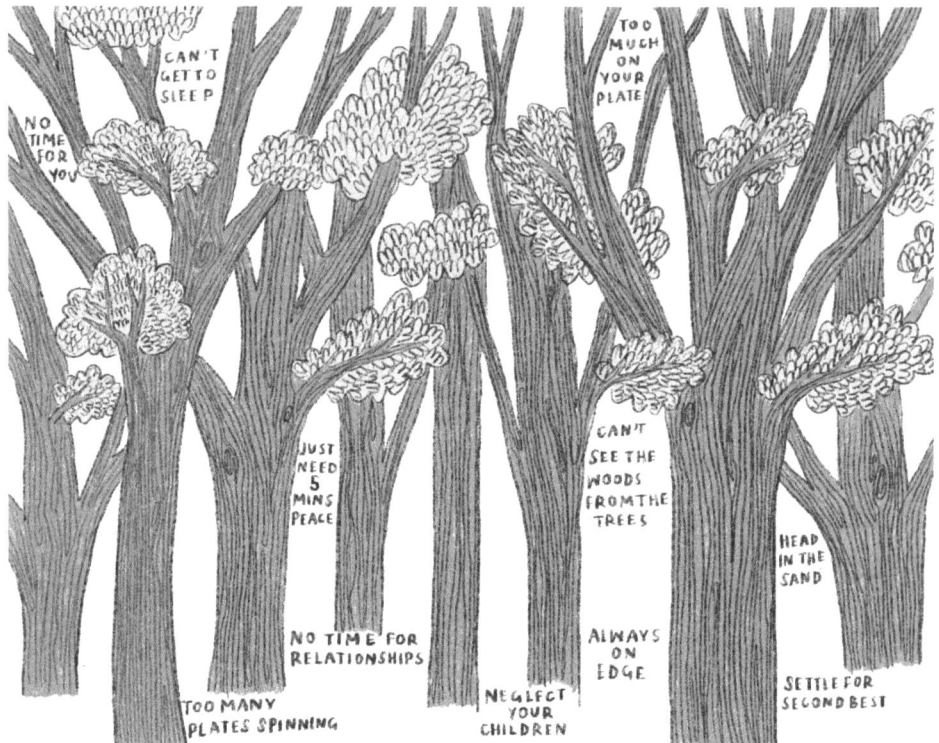

CB4: Incidentals

In truth, there are all manner of reasons we can think of to avoid doing things – or avoid not doing things. Of course, they're not actually legitimate reasons: sound arguments for a considered course of action. They're just emotional avoidance strategies. We contrive an excuse to escape something we don't like the look of, the sound of or feel like. They're psychological get-out clauses and can be dredged from many different dubious origins.

*   *Historical: my mother always used to say….*
    We selectively employ the wisdom of our forebearers and ancestors when it suits. My Dad always used to say, 'if it ain't broke, don't fix it…'. Not only do we generate a reason not to pursue improvement, we convince ourselves that it would be an act of betrayal. We're actually paying homage to our elders by respecting the advice. We're upholding a legacy.

*   *Circumstantial: the wind's getting up…*
    If we look hard enough, there is always a reason to put off doing something. It can be too hot, too cold, too wet, too windy, too early, too late – you name it. We know the excuse is a lame excuse, but we provide ourselves with just enough 'plausible deniability' to extricate ourselves from what we should really be engaging with. Of course, there's never a right time.

    We decide to start our health kick on Monday, because that's the start of a new working week, and makes more sense than in the middle of the weekend (obviously). Or there's no point contemplating a new project over the Christmas season; we save that for a New Year's Resolution. And we all know how they work out. There are always numerous spurious reasons for postponing even the smallest adjustment, if you look hard enough.

*   *Catastrophic: it's all getting a bit too much…*
    Worrying about what the future may hold usually paints the scariest possible picture. When we're threatened, we hunker down and surround ourselves with the familiar. We cling on to our tried-and-tested habits, practices and places like a routine comfort blanket. Only it's exactly that: a blanket, not a shield.

> **Catastrophic behaviours only foreshorten our horizons, as we peep at the world from under the bed covers.**

All closed behaviours can only be tackled with an open mind. An open mind requires opening; like a fire door, our minds are constantly endeavouring to shut. Closing our personal borders to anyone – anything – is our natural defensive default position. Receptivity counters long-standing cemented beliefs, and inches open the closed doors that curtail our potential. Receptivity is a wedge under the door. It works, but it requires a little effort and positioning. Occasionally, it benefits from a kick at just the right time. In simple terms, receptivity is about being up for it. It means going against the grain and keeping on going. It takes effort and sometimes imagination. It takes consistency and stubbornness. But most of all, it's all about one thing.

It's all about finding your floss.

Chapter 7

Receptivity: Finding Your Floss

Firstly, a word about the birds. Not in the Alfred Hitchcock, sense. I'm talking the dawn chorus: the avian equivalent of the Last Night of the Proms. Only more 'first light of the morning' than 'last night'. It is, for want of a better word, a 'thing'. Each day, weather permitting, where there's birdlife, there's hope. A new day, a new dawn, a random and sizeable *a capello* ensemble burst in to spontaneous song. It's a joy to behold and never fails to deliver. The birds perform with unbridled gusto and abandon.

Every day really is a brand-new day. Our feathered friends are genuinely excited when night finally draws to an end and the sun miraculously puts in a reappearance. You suspect when darkness descends the birds really wonder whether the end is nigh. A new dawn is welcomed with a mixture of relief and unbridled jubilation; the birds get to do it all again. Existence is celebrated with unrestrained joy once more. In a world where anything can happen, the worst hasn't – far from it - and that's a wonderful thing. The birds are grateful to be alive. A fresh start, a blank canvas lays before them. They're back in the game, the right sort of a flap.

They don't sweat the small stuff. They don't turn over and go back to sleep, hoping to 'snooze' life. They don't begin clock-watching and counting down. They don't start grumbling about the morning commute. They are early, never late, showing up as soon as they can to make the very most of the new day. They don't save it for the weekend.

What do they do? They fly the nest every single day, the ultimate leap of faith. Sure, there's risk. They're not guaranteed a soft landing. There are cats. The weather can take a turn for the worst. They're often flying on a wing and a prayer. There's always a bigger bird waiting in the wings to attempt a hostile takeover bid for the nest.

Sometimes all of the above happens and stuff goes wrong.
Sometimes all of the above happens and stuff goes right.

Sometimes none of the above happens and stuff goes wrong.
Sometimes none of the above happens and stuff goes right.

Which all goes to show there are never ever any guarantees.

> **We can live in fear of the worst things that can possibly happen, but that is not really living at all. Alternatively, we can live in such a way that opens the door to the possibility that the best just might happen.**

The former is a non-starter: choosing despair in the hope that there will be no unpleasant surprises. Unfortunately, lowering your expectations doesn't actually elevate your experience. Yes, you're not surprised when things go badly but this eventually begins to morph into grim expectation. We create our own negative self-fulfilling prophecies. We become very good at looking for signs that everything is going pear-shaped and, unsurprisingly, tend to find some. More than most.

Receptivity is the bedrock of unconscious incompetence. The capacity to remain open-minded outside your comfort zone is key to personal development. Being comfortable with what you're getting into without knowing what it is admittedly takes practice. Rather than having 'blind faith' I would describe this as maintaining a positive outlook.

The dawn chorus

Being more 'dawn chorus' is about being up for whatever the day's got in store. It's something that we can all learn, but I also suspect that it's something that many people have also unlearnt. Growing older doesn't necessarily mean wiser. With years come veneers. We cultivate various facades to try to placate the world around us. At home and at work, we endeavour to do the right thing which often translates to the popular thing. The trouble is that popular 'received' wisdom is not always wise. It is, however, easier – at least in the short term. Popular wisdom is generally acceptable, but that doesn't mean it's not painful nevertheless.

If the majority of people complain about being stuck in a dead-end job, we tend to accept that's just how it is. We grow to assume it's normal to spend the majority of our waking hours feeling unfulfilled and implicitly begrudging of life. The easiest option is to blame everyone and anyone for the predicament we find ourselves in. The more challenging option is to actually do something about it. The trouble with accepting responsibility, is that it significantly limits the number of people available to blame. There is ultimately only one person left to turn to: you. That doesn't stop us trying to pin the blame elsewhere, however.

Social media has turned venting into an art form. There are so many ways to pour scorn on people, places, circumstance and situation, we're always just a few clicks away from an argument. It's easy to get drawn into the melee.

Life can be a grisly spectacle. Bad things do happen, are happening and unfortunately will continue to happen – sometimes close to home. But the more digging we engage in, the more dirt we unearth and the more of a mess we create.

It is possible to make good things happen. Passivity – not making – leaves a vacuum which is quickly filled with the toxicity of others. Unfortunately, it is far easier to pour scorn on others than hold yourself accountable.

> **Making a positive difference requires adopting an insistent and persistent mindset, urgently understanding that life is there for the taking and the making.**

If you're genuinely prepared to put your mind, body and soul into it, opportunities present to materialise change for the better. You need to fully commit.

Commitment might entail…

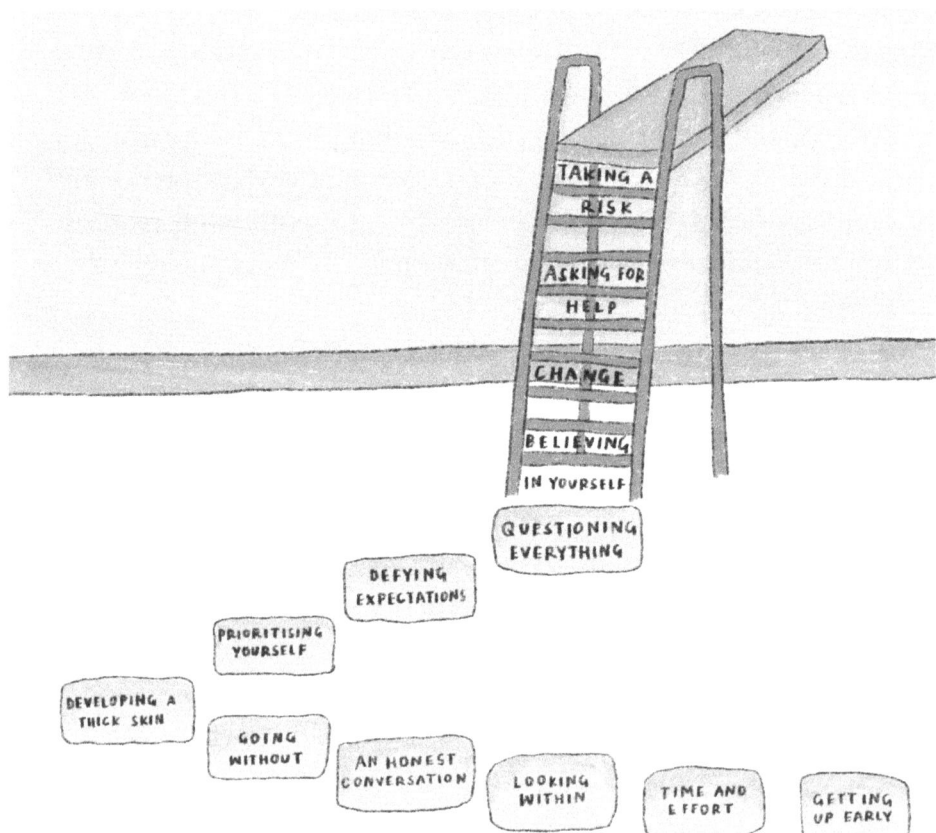

Resilience 2.0: Embracing Challenge and Change

Let's talk about Teddy

At only five years old, he can't exactly be described as worldly-wise, but he's most definitely wise beyond his years. Teddy is my next-door neighbour, a fizzing concentration of energy bundled into a knitted tank top. Every day is not just a new day, but it's a brand-new day, bringing all the promise and excitement shiny new things do. Teddy is my go-to guy when it comes to a lesson in receptivity. He is the personification of receptivity.

Not too long ago, I was wandering down the garden path at the end of the day. Framed by next door's loft conversion, I spied Teddy (or rather he spied me) waving excitedly. Whilst this wasn't unusual for Teddy, even by his standards, he seemed to be particularly animated on this occasion. His Mum was less so, who from a distance managed to look somewhat embarrassed. I assumed she'd not long stepped out of the shower, as she had a wet towel wrapped around her head. Teddy, however, would not be deterred from his mission. His enthusiasm would not be dampened. His Mum had him firmly secured by the scruff of the neck, just in case he jumped 'out of his skin' and inadvertently out of the window.

As I got closer still, I could see that Teddy appeared to be holding something in his hands. 'Will!' he shouted, 'Will. LOOK!' Look I did and couldn't see a thing. Further explanation was required. It was soon forthcoming.

'Look, Will! Look! Dental floss,' he shouted, 'I'VE GOT DENTAL FLOSS!' And sure enough, he did. Teddy had just been inducted into the weird and wonderful world of oral hygiene. He was excited, to say the least, brandishing an almost invisible silver slither of floss. I made what I considered to be suitably approving sentiments conveying my awe and wonder, validated with a thumbs-up, before retreating to the familiar humdrum of the kitchen.

Whilst removing my shoes, I gave a chuckle accompanied by a short shake of the head, reflecting on Teddy's exuberance. Stopping mid-shake, the realisation began to dawn. Maybe Teddy was on to something. Maybe dental floss was about more than cleaning teeth, it was about our ability to smile. Maybe 'flossing' is key to being receptive. Maybe flossing is receptivity in action.

The world is neutral

The world doesn't have political leanings. It doesn't have an opinion on the weather; it just rains, snows or shines and repeats. The water-cycle is on a continuous automatic loop. The world really doesn't care how you feel, but you should. Because on a bad day, the whole world is against you, and on a good day, you can do no wrong.

Take a moment to think about a 'bad' day. One of those days when everything that seemingly could go wrong, does. We fear that it's going to be 'one of those days' fairly early on, as something untoward happens (flat tyre, the cat's been sick, you name it) which seemingly sets the tone for what is to follow. The warning signs are there. Here we go again…. We mentally adopt the brace position.

'Setting the tone' is part of the problem, however. The tone can be more to do with the 'setting' than the actual tone. More direction than substance. Set off on the wrong footing, and we're soon plummeting in a spiralling trajectory and inadvertently contriving to create – and pursue – a self-fulfilling prophecy. Because our mood and interactions are a negative reflection of, and reaction to, our experiences thus far, things have a tendency to go from bad to worse. And from worse to worser. Our bad mood means we don't hide our frustrations, responding and reacting badly to whatever follows. We're a little impatient with family, friends or colleagues, meaning their subsequent reactions aren't favourable. We contrive a grey cloud that hangs over us all day, casting a gloomy shadow on whatever and whoever we encounter. It doesn't end well because it didn't start well.

Resilience 2.0: Embracing Challenge and Change

Teddy is not a grey cloud, however, he's the opposite. Teddy is a ray of sunshine. He's a flamingo in a flock of pigeons. He sets off on the right footing. In fact, he puts his best foot firmly forwards. Every day is a new day and he's up for it. Whatever the day brings, he has the innate capacity to generate some excitement about the prospect of what's to come. Every day, Teddy asks himself 'what's the best that can happen?'. When it comes to being receptive, we can all learn a thing or two from Teddy.

Everyone has a floss. Many of us have more than one. We don't always register it, but we do. Those of us who think we don't, just haven't acknowledged it yet. A 'floss' is something that gets you ready for the day; that helps you get 'up' for it. Call it what you will – getting your act together, making some headroom, becoming centred – flossing is what it is. That particular routine, activity or practice that helps you get into the zone. It's a personal primer, your Resilience 2.0 upgrade in action.

If you're in the zone, you're much better placed to deal with whatever the day has in store for you. You're ready for it. This 'bring-it-on' attitude is essentially the positivity required to nudge your day in an upwards trajectory. Rather than waiting for the day, it's making the day; cajoling the good. Flossing overcomes the inertia of waking-up slightly groggy and catapults you forwards. When you're on an upwards trajectory, it's going to take something significant to bring you down. When you're on a downwards trajectory, remember, it's an effort just to get out of bed in the morning. When you're down, you stay down.

> **Flossing helps you to get high, legally.**

A floss might only look – and feel – like a floss to you and only you. From the outside, it could merely be viewed as an insignificance: a distraction or even an irritation. An unnecessary and unwarranted interruption. It's far from it. It's a powerful transformative tool, a catalyst for sparking your day. A psychological tinder box. It's an essential cornerstone ritual for maintaining a healthy, happy, functioning you. Your floss, or combination of flosses, is unique to you. Other people's might appeal to you, but what really works for you is often a combination of trial-and-error, personal to your particular set of circumstances. Here are two contrasting examples.

A. Dishwashing

My two children seem to have a blind spot for the dishwasher. It appears to be a glaring absence that defies the laws of physics. I've reached this judgement after years of futile attempts in schooling two children in how to load and unload the dishwasher. Not necessarily 'loading and unloading the dishwasher' correctly, even. A token insertion would be acceptable. Sadly, all to no avail.

If left for a whole day, the assorted detritus multiplies exponentially into startling proportions and configurations, threatening to irretrievably Jenga at any moment. Returning home to a precarious kitchen is never easy and fraught with danger.

Emptying the dishwasher in the morning is a floss. If the sides are clear and the dishwasher is empty, I can embark upon whatever the day has in store for me, safe in the knowledge that I've done everything humanly possible to avert a kitchen catastrophe. I've made peace with the kitchen. Clear dishwasher means clarity of mind.

If I don't empty the dishwasher, the potential carnage I might return home to means the balance of the day has already started to tip against me. An almost imperceptible anxiousness creeps into my thoughts and behaviour, and already the day becomes something of an uphill battle. Alternatively, if the dishwasher is empty, I'm winning. It's a small win, but a win, nevertheless.

B. Running

Running is my chosen form of exercise. I'm aware that not everyone exercises, and not everyone has a chosen 'form,' but running is the one that works for me. It works on a number of levels. Firstly, it helps to offset my considerable penchant for cake. Secondly, I enjoy being outside in all seasons. In fact, I enjoy running because of the seasons; it gives me an appreciation of the changing weather and environment, all of which provide a rich immersive experience. In other words, I feel like I'm in the thick of it. I notice things evolve. Things are sown, grown, ripen, harvested and repeated. And then there's the 'after-run'. When it's cold, I enjoy a hot cup of tea afterwards. When it's hot, I enjoy something cold afterwards (and a hot cup of tea). Even when the weather is horrible, sometimes because the weather is horrible, I get a primal satisfaction in enduring, overcoming and subsequently recuperating afterwards. It feels like a challenge overcome. I've risen to that challenge.

Thirdly, I feel physically better. A little more alive and a little less creaky. I use bits that otherwise would seldom get used (I don't even run to catch a bus anymore). We've got mechanisms, levers and joints that are designed for propulsion. It's what we were intended to do. If you don't use it, you lose it.

Fourthly, running gives me a precious segment of time all to myself which isn't interrupted by emails, dogs or children. It feels like it's good for my headspace, because it ringfences that very space. It's time for me. Putting one foot in front of the other repeatedly, strips away accumulated brain fug.

Running is WD40 for my soul.

Putting your best foot forwards

If you want to put the world in perspective, I strongly recommend buying a pair of running shoes. There's something about the simple act of putting one foot in front of another repeatedly that initiates a cleansing meditative state. It's an uncomplicated remedy to modern life. You become slightly removed from reality, focusing primarily upon your breathing and the act of putting one foot in front of another, again and again and again…. I guess it's a form of mindfulness (or mind emptiness). After a mile or so, you find a rhythm. Your body's natural rhythm. You literally fall in to step with the machinations of existence. Breathing in and out. Finding this state transcends the immediacy and emergency of whatever was pressing hitherto. Trials and tribulations pale into insignificance whilst you regain perspective, focusing upon inhaling and exhaling.

Our lives are predominantly spent careering around at full speed attempting to squeeze in more and more. We try to occupy ourselves from dawn until dusk, as though we're actually frightened of stopping to take a breath. We're scared of what a little introspection might reveal. Rather than deal with a toxic work dynamic or address spiralling credit card bills, for instance, we choose to carry on regardless, or distract ourselves by getting on with something else. This pseudo stoicism is not ignorance, however. We know, deep down, of the damage we are doing.

> **We *do* more and more and more to distract us from having to consider how to *be* more. Rather than deal with the challenges of the moment, we duck them.**

The 'running' state of detachment proves to be a very creative one. If you've got problems to solve, being slightly removed from them helps you to think and see more clearly. By putting your best foot forward you've achieved the ability to take a step back and take stock afresh. Even if you haven't got problems to solve, the creative space you

Resilience 2.0: Embracing Challenge and Change

inhabit when running derives solutions. Things click, ideas spark and hair-brained schemes begin to materialise. The exercised mind is a creative space, a place of betterment.

I benefit hugely from running. Some of those benefits are real and some just 'feel' real, which I guess might make them actually real. Regardless, going for a run – not necessarily very far or very fast – means I feel up for the day. I've made the effort to invest in myself and prepare for whatever the day has in store.

Substitute running for walking, gardening, washing the car, chopping firewood – whatever. Exercise your right to exercise.

It's worth noting that a floss does not have to be a morning practice; any time of the day works, just so long as it works for you. Some people opt for hitting the gym on their way home from work, for example. Others value a lunchtime stroll in the park. You may well have multiple flosses, providing positive benchmarks throughout the day.

It's easy to ignore the importance of your floss because it's optional. It's an additional extra that doesn't need to be fitted in, yet is immensely beneficial, none the less. Flossing is the key to personal receptivity. When you're up for it, not only do you benefit, but so does everyone around you. They get the very best of you and the very best from you.

Flosses are very personal both in nature and combination. You might enjoy a coffee in bed in the morning whilst tackling the day's crossword. That seemingly simple floss has multiple layers: the bed, the coffee, exercising and priming the brain. It might not be everyone's cup of tea (or coffee) but it works for some of us. It helps us get up out of bed rather than just get out of bed. If you're going to rise, you might as well shine.

Flossing might be…

p	o	l	i	s	h	i	n	g	c	a	r
r					a				u		
a			d		n		s		p		c
y	o	g	a		g		t		o		h
e			n		i		i		f		o
r			c		n		l		t		c
			e		g		l		e		o
					o		n		a		l
					u		e				a
	f	r	u	i	t		s				t
g					w		s				e
a					a						
m		b	i	n	s	o	u	t		s	
e					h					h	
					i					a	
r	e	a	d	i	n	g	b	o	o	k	
					g					e	

Child's play

Children are very good at exploring the art of flossing. They are constantly prospecting: panning for gold, mining for practices that provide some sort of fulfilment, fillip or boost. Whether it's the sensory stimulation of making mud pies, the excitement of shinning up a tree or the satisfaction of camping in a home-made den, kids are adept at sourcing their mental and physical nourishment. The older we get, unfortunately, we learn to displace such practices (and the pursuit of) with inferior adult pastimes. Some of these are ineffectual, some even destructive. Many are rather dull. We open another bottle of wine rather than do something. We scroll to the detriment of our own physical activity. We learn to mimic the circuitous behaviours of others, feeding and compounding a need to do more of the same. We go round and round in pointless pursuit, at the expense of developing ourselves, our unique individual passions, interests, dreams and vocations. At the expense of finding our own way. Rather than galvanise, we calcify.

> **Flossing is a small-but-perfectly-formed first step towards rekindling your lust for life.**

It's about reclaiming that special thing that makes you, you. It's a gentle push factor, moving you towards being the sort of person you want to be, by doing the things you want to do. The things that make you tick. The things that you rate, and in turn, rating yourself. You are worthy.

Chapter 8
The Scab of Contentment

Receptivity requires a push, but also benefits from a pull. Something that attracts you. A motivation that drives you towards an alternative vision. An alternative – whether that's in our professional lives, personal lives, or any combination of – is a powerful igniting force. The majority of us don't do 'alternative'. We are cemented in 'sameness'. Rather than countenance possibility, we fester in familiarity.

Status woe

We don't necessarily enjoy the status quo, it's just easier to stay put rather than put ourselves out. Many people openly despise the way things are, yet will only countenance temporary sticking-plaster solutions. Pangs of dissatisfaction can temporarily be subdued by selecting from a vast array of readily available distractions. Alcohol, pornography, drugs, shopping, social media – to name but a few – can all be accessed with frightening ease in the modern inter-connected world. We offset our discontentment and disillusionment by substitution. Unfortunately, such escapism makes the shock upon returning to 'reality' even more acute.

'Sticking plasters' are only a temporary remedy because they provide a short, sharp spike of relief. They don't make things better: just briefly stop them from feeling any worse. Consider purchasing a pair of new shoes, for example.

> The shoes look good, sound good, even smell good. You visualise yourself wearing them and they make you look good! You are soon the proud owner of a brand-new pair of shoes and have an extra spring in your step. For a short time, at least.

The novelty starts wearing off surprisingly quickly. You wear them a few times, and the new shoes aren't new, anymore. They're not put away quite so carefully and have to take their chances with the rest of the shoe cupboard. That initial spike of excitement you felt upon purchasing your shoes has, well… spiked. It's been and gone. You were up and now you're down. Again.

So, you look for a substitute shoe-fix. It could be another pair of shoes, but your conscious mind might struggle with the blatant absurdity of that, so maybe you deserve a meal out, instead? Or perhaps a holiday? Or you deserve a new bag and a meal out on holiday? Surely, you ask yourself, I can justify spending on something, regardless of whether you can actually afford it?! You deserve it, after all…

The shoe purchase reflects our fickle pursuit of happiness. It's not the shoes that float our boat, but the way we think about our shoes, and the fleeting shot of dopamine this provides. If it really was the shoes that were key to sustained elevated feelings of wellbeing, surely that feeling would last just as long as the shoes do? We all know, of course, that we're soon craving another pair – or another something – long before a visit to the cobblers is required. Come to think of it, how many of us visit the cobblers these days, anyway?! Shoe happiness is a load of cobblers; it's really not about the shoes.

And so, we lurch from scratching one itch to another, all the while exacerbating the underlying problem. Humans are great at picking the scab of discontent. We don't need any more superficial distractions; we need to stop scratching. We need a purpose.

A purpose generates long-term receptivity

A purpose audits your time, adding value to your existence. It ignites an inner drive that replaces yearning with channelled momentum. Momentum moves you. It moves you away from one thing and towards another. A purpose helps you to be open to the right sort of change, moving in the right sort of direction, at a speed that makes you feel alive. It helps you feel fulfilled.

Purpose is an ace in a world where we stick or twist. Shy of change, our default setting is to stick, hoping we'll stay in the game. Purpose upgrades the hand that you play with, improving your chances of winning in life.

Perhaps the most important thing to bear in mind about purpose, is that like flossing, it's uniquely personal in nature. It sits at the opposite end of the 'spike of happiness' spectrum. Rather than a quick fix, purpose is not readily obtainable, but resonates much more deeply. It's a high-hanging fruit. Authentic 'purpose' is challenging to reach and requires a significant amount of investment. It's a stretch, by any measure. It is, however, 'real' and lasting.

By 'real' I mean that it's not just a pipe dream. That doesn't mean it can't be on the edges of achievability, just that you've got to be able to align yourself with the possibility of fulfilment. Without visualisation, it's impossible to invest the time and effort required. Pipe dreams are not authentic goals, they're just a convenient excuse for not pursuing genuine change. A pipe dream that might involve, for instance, starting a new life on a tropical island, is conveniently unrealistic for all of us who don't genuinely want to entertain the possibility that we can make a difference. We file it under the 'nice thought' category and then continue with the humdrum everyday, wistfully sidestepping any opportunity for improvement. And the responsibility required to initiate genuine change. Pipe dreams give purpose a bad name; they bundle all aspirations into the bracket of delusional. Only the deluded would waste time pursuing the impossible, after all.

A goal that is linked to your purpose should be a stretch – perhaps even an impossible stretch – but not subconsciously contrived to be unobtainable. If you don't buy in to it, you're never going to genuinely invest in it. It might sound strange that people set goals which they don't genuinely believe in, but it actually makes perfect sense. Not investing emotionally into a particular venture, whatever it might be, nullifies the risk of disappointment. If you don't really believe that something is possible, if you've never really subscribed to it, it's not such a big deal when it doesn't happen. We shrug our shoulders and move on to the next whim. Serial pipe dreamers might seem like they've forever got their head in the clouds, but actually their feet are planted firmly on the ground. Unfortunately, being rooted to the spot never gets you anywhere.

I'm not suggesting your purpose should be rigidly defined by statistical chances of success; if that were the case nobody would ever overcome the odds of adversity. People do go from rags-to-riches, after all – just that you have to identify with it. Your purpose is something that pushes you, pulls you and stirs you.

> **Without emotion there will be no motion – and purpose is designed to move you – to be a catalyst for behaviour change.**

Just to be clear, wholeheartedly committing to your purpose, goal, aim, target, destination – whatever you want to call it – does not in any way guarantee you'll achieve it. It does, however, mean you are far more likely to take significant steps towards it. You're in with a chance. Progress towards aspiration creates a momentum that fuels changes in behaviour, attitudes and outcomes. Rather than the fleeting high that's felt with a new purchase, we experience a deeper, longer-lasting feeling of fulfilment. Fulfilment is the self-charging equivalence of receptivity. It's sustainable because it's cumulative and generative; every step you take towards your goal is banked and built upon. For every day that you invest in pursuing your purpose, you are fuelled by that pursuit. In the same way that exercise contributes to more fitness rather than less, the sense of fulfilment you feel from working towards something authentic gets stronger and stronger.

A purpose is an excellent way of helping you to fire on all cylinders. Firing on all cylinders means that you are genuinely receptive, ready for whatever excitement the day might bring, embracing unconscious incompetence because you possess direction. Purpose pushes you out of the fug of sameness, stretching your comfort zone and shaking up routine. Purposeful actions form the bedrock of a good day. You know that whatever comes your way, you've already added to the foundations of personal betterment. Purpose isn't easy.

Purpose is …

Small steps

To really move you, purpose is distilled into bite-size daily actions. These petit purposes are the necessary building blocks of your resilient journey, instilling behaviours that transform the seemingly uneventful to productive, fulfilling and rewarding. The rewards are felt as soon as you engage with the behaviours, regardless of whether or not your purpose has technically been 'achieved'. Achievement is a lot further down the line, at least to begin with.

If my purpose is to run a marathon, I need a plan of incremental tangible actions. This is what they could look like:

✳ Google 'marathon'
✳ Count to 26 (.2)
✳ Try going for a run
✳ Try walking further than a mile
✳ Purchase a pair of running trainers
✳ Have my gait analysed
✳ Receive a medical check-up
✳ Download a beginner's training plan
✳ Source some running kit
✳ Try running at different times of the day
✳ Remember to walk before you run
✳ Schedule when to run
✳ Run
✳ Consider using an app to help record and measure relevant data
✳ Decide whether to upgrade to the full paid version
✳ Stretch every day
✳ Consider joining a running club
✳ Wear a headband
✳ Research a healthy, balanced diet
✳ Reward yourself with cake
✳ Join an online running community
✳ Run a race that isn't a marathon. In fact, run lots of them.

Every bite-size action can be further divided into even more digestible sub-behaviours. 'Source some running kit', for instance, may be more than the one-stop-shop that it may at first appear. It may, in fact, require frequenting multiple shops and online providers of running apparel.

Sourcing the running kit may consist of:

* Digging out an old pair of shorts and trying them on for size
* Throwing away aforementioned old pair of shorts
* Comparing a handful of different online sportswear retailers
* Contemplating appropriate garments for the weather
* Considering how to keep your hair out of your eyes
* Ruminating over specialist running socks: are they really necessary?

Each action or 'sub-action' is the physical manifestation of purpose. Remember; purpose is the 'Pushmepullyou' of receptivity, driving you forwards on a positive trajectory.

> **The golden rule of receptivity is to undertake an action every single day that is in alignment with your purpose.**

Receptivity tasks are sacred; they must be scheduled into your day and ringfenced, giving them sufficient priority and every opportunity to transpire. This might sound – and feel – something of a drag to begin with, which is why initially every effort must be taken to ensure it happens. This conscious 'effort' is your friend and key to building transformational momentum. Over time, conscious application becomes automatic as your deliberate actions become woven seamlessly into the fabric of daily life.

If you can string a handful of days together using this mechanism, you have effectively created a 'purpose streak'. The streak becomes less of a drag, and each subsequent action becomes easier due to the slipstreaming effect. Just like there is a sweet spot of 'clean air' if you follow closely behind a bicycle, so to with task engagement. There is less turbulence involved. Your cumulative efforts have overcome the initial inertia required to 'get started' and you are on a roll. Indeed, the momentum will reach a stage when it's harder not to pursue your purpose because you have become sucked in. More effort is now required to do less than to do more. Effort becomes effortless.

This tipping point can be reached sooner than you think but depends upon the '3 Ps': the Person, the Purpose and the extent of the Progress.

The person
Some people take a little longer to get fired up than others. Some people's fires are more glowing embers than raging infernos. The more fired up you become, the more quickly you get excited about purpose pursuit, but also run the risk of burning out more rapidly. By contrast, a fire that barely burns is susceptible to dampened enthusiasm.

Somewhere in between the two is ideal; neither incendiary nor a damp squib. We all know people who throw themselves wholeheartedly into a new venture, usually accompanied by a sizeable outlay of cash and with great fanfare, who lose interest just as quickly. They fizzle out and lose impetus because they've not first cemented the building blocks of receptivity. Enthusiasm has spiked, building rapidly before becoming suppressed by a disheartening apparent lack of progress. This 'all or nothing' approach usually ends up with nothing. A more measured approach is what's required. Throwing yourself wholeheartedly into a new venture isn't necessarily a bad thing, just so long as the throw is controlled.

Some degree of emotional buy-in is essential. Without emotion there is no motion, and progress will stall like a car that's struggling to select the right gear. Passivity gets you nowhere very quickly, purpose requires some degree of drive to get anywhere.

The purpose

Remember, purpose is a key tenet of receptivity. It's got to resonate in some way. A person must be prepared to 'let go' and allow themselves to feel energised. This is much easier with a purpose that shakes things up. Purpose provides meaning, direction – and importantly – a tingle of excitement. 'Tingling' is not an exact science.

Personally, flying to Mars doesn't provide me with a tingle. Not because it wouldn't be an out-of-this-world amazing experience, but because it's an unrealistic dream. Deep down, I know it's almost an impossibility. It's practically impossible. That's not defeatist; it's merely being realistic. The honest truth is you cannot do anything you want to do or be anyone you want to be. Pretending otherwise is at best counter-productive and worst borderline delusional. Not only do you not even come close to achieving your dream, it undermines the confidence to pursue future projects. Because you've previously fallen a long way short, it's easy to negatively extrapolate. Your track record can be a hindrance. Your purpose should be big, but practically obtainable.

The progress

The importance of progress cannot be overstated as is the recognition of that progress. Some people are reluctant to acknowledge their successes, for fear of over-egging the pudding. Playing down our progress is a mechanism we all employ to some extent, tempering our enthusiasm and optimism to soften the potential blow of any future disappointment. There's nothing wrong with measuring perspective and not getting carried away, just so long as you don't overdo it. Or perhaps – more accurately – under do it. Too much restraint leads to self-handicapping and creates unnecessary developmental drag. The truth of the matter is we all need small victories, and we all need to register them. Without some sort of validation, it's nigh on impossible to maintain any meaningful positive momentum.

Your progress matters, no matter how small or insignificant it may seem. It's important to acknowledge the strides you make and celebrate them appropriately and accordingly. That might mean quietly confiding in a trusted friend or it could mean a smug ten minutes of self-congratulatory private reflection, patting yourself on the back with a cup of tea and a custard cream.

In essence, you are rewarding yourself for being one of the relatively few who act, rather than the many who talk. Talk is cheap. Don't allow the empty broadcasts of others to undermine your genuine effort and endeavour, however small or insignificant it might initially seem. Good practice trumps good intentions every time.

Action is what facilitates genuine improvement. Without action, all you are left with is mental trickery and mind games: cajoling yourself to see things differently to how they actually are. Action breeds further action.

> **Receptivity is a mixture of attitude and application. A positive mindset alone is nothing but pleasant smoke-and-mirrors; it quickly disperses and only works in a certain light. It requires substance.**

Action without conscious direction is similarly doomed. It's the proverbial headless chicken: frenetically going nowhere and achieving very little. Headless chickens are found in every workplace. People who constantly broadcast about how much they have to do and how little time they have to do it, rather than actually engaging with any meaningful tasks. These are the very same presentees who credit being first in to work and the last to leave, confusing attendance with productivity. Headless chickens are not just harmless characters with misguided enthusiasm, however. They contaminate the culture of a workplace by the mismatch between words and deeds, often skewing the attitudes and appreciation of others.

Loudly professing to be one thing where evidence suggests the contrary causes confusion, irritation and resentment amongst colleagues. Sometimes headless chickens broadcast more subtly, spreading their doctrine by whispered inference. This is the most dangerous and damaging type as it is harder to consciously defend against. With more overt broadcasting, the contradiction is clear for all to see, the visibility diluting its impact. The more subtle variety goes under the radar and sews the seeds of dissonance. A disgruntled workforce is the result, who then set about seeking justification for their gripes and grievances.

Receptivity is the DNA of change, the nucleus of challenge. We have to work hard to find it in the right places. It's not a passive pursuit, but a trait to be proactively created and curated. Waiting doesn't work. There is never a right time. When you are genuinely up for it, it's time to cultivate the second key tenet of resilience. It's time to brave it.

It's time to risk it.

Chapter 9

Risk

> **Life is a risky business. The whole of it. An eighty-year gamble that may or may not pay off. It may be longer, and it may be shorter, which all adds to the jeopardy.**

Living requires continually weighing the potential risks of our thoughts, actions or inaction with the likely consequences. And there are *always* consequences. Choosing not to act doesn't eliminate consequence, it merely defaults to an alternative. Doing nothing doesn't mean nothing changes, it just means your influence diminishes. The changes determine you, rather than you them. Someone else rolls the dice whilst you hope for a seven.

Many people confuse inaction with maintaining the status quo. Inaction – standing still – whilst the world continues to turn, affects the equilibrium in just the same way as electing to take a particular course. Whether you opt to stick or twist, the risk remains the same. In a changing world you either get ahead or get left behind. Risk is inevitable because the juxtaposition between your current existence and the future is constantly shifting. It requires adjustment one way or another.

Risk simply cannot be avoided. It's ever present. Everywhere we go, everything we do, contains the potential for mishap, mayhem and miscalculation. At this very moment, as you read this sentence, you are not immune from risk. There is a chance (albeit small) of a rather unsettling encounter with an escaped tiger from the local zoo, for instance. Or maybe there's a risk that it might rain. On the spectrum of certainty and impossibility, most events fall somewhere in between both poles. There's always a chance that something will go right – or wrong. Upgrading your resilience requires significantly upgrading your risk threshold. Navigating unconscious incompetence – knowing what needs to be done but not knowing how to do it – means exploring unchartered territory. Anything can happen.

Risk avoidance is really offsetting risk. We either postpone dealing with risky business (which may exacerbate the risk) or attempt to neutralise the potential consequences. Risk is only managed and manipulated, never completely eliminated. A life without risk simply does not exist, yet many people are still in pursuit of such a promised land. There is an unknown quantity about risk. Human beings crave certainty. The unknown quantity is often where the risk originates.

Unknowns include:

Resilience 2.0: Embracing Challenge and Change

Risky combinations

Risk is an abstract concept. Many things are not risky in isolation, but a series of unfortunate events that conspire to create a perfect storm. An unfortunate series of events is often a string of benign incidents whose juxtaposition contrives jeopardy. The events are often non-descript in isolation, innocuous signposts on the way to something unpredictable and impactful. It is our choices – the directions we take – upon encountering such signposts that seal our fate when managing risk. Failure to deal with risk is the biggest risk.

Fear of risk is often disproportionate to the magnitude of danger that presents. Small risks can create significant overreaction, such as an aversion to spiders, for instance. Overreaction in itself can elevate the actual risk, as heightened reactions and exaggerated behaviours can cause secondary consequences.

Conversely, the well-documented risks of drinking, smoking, over-eating and inactivity, for instance, are very real. Despite significant danger to our health, some people seem relatively unperturbed and even dismissive. Coronary disease poses significantly more of a threat than a common or garden spider, yet our attitudes, responses and behaviours are somewhat muted. Our attitude to risk management is wildly inconsistent. In other words, we don't manage it.

We fear what might come to pass and risk exposing ourselves to that fear. Risk can exist without fear (you can be blissfully unaware, for instance, of that faulty wiring) and fear exists without risk (honestly, there isn't a monster hiding under your bed). Sometimes our biggest fears are completely unfounded and mere figments of our imagination. That doesn't make them feel any less real, however.

It is possible to function successfully in a climate of extreme fear. Elite special forces soldiers are trained to operate effectively in situations that are both extremely dangerous and frightening. Fear exists, the dangers and risks are very real and careful handling is required.

The trick is to be more Indiana Jones. That's right: intrepid explorer, archaeologist and defender of rare and priceless artefacts and antiquities. Think action, adventure and fedora. He may be a fictional character, but it's a fact we can all learn from his fearless exploits. Namely, how to deal with risk and fear.

Picture Professor Henry Jones in an archetypal scenario: some sort of tight spot in pursuance of hitherto hidden treasure. Getting his hands on the prize is only half the battle, getting out alive is the real challenge now. A potentially catastrophic chain reaction is accidentally set in motion, with poison arrows, enormous barrelling boulders and all manner of hazards trying to snare our intrepid explorer upon his hastened exit. Invariably, he makes it just in the nick of time, hurling himself through the slenderest of gaps, escaping just before a huge stone slab seals his fate forever.

…But not before dislodging his beloved hat in the process. Just when we think it's lost for good, Indie reaches behind and retrieves it with a flourish, but only just. A fraction of a second later, and his arm would have been pinned to the floor for ever more. He was taking a risk, and an unnecessary one, at that.

The question is why? What's with the hat? Why risk your life for the sake of a hat?

Sure, it might be a special hat; maybe a family heirloom, passed down through successive generations of Joneses. Maybe it's got sentimental value. Maybe it's an expensive hat, woven from the finest threads of ancient Persia. Maybe, but I reckon not. The hat has something more about it than mere monetary value or familial history.

Resilience 2.0: Embracing Challenge and Change

Indiana Jones' hat enables him to be Indiana Jones.

It is an essential part of his identity, imbibing him with his intrepid qualities. Without his fedora he is merely Professor Henry Jones – a man limited to finding his way around an encyclopaedia – his expertise purely academic. Indie's hat is instrumental in his transformation from mild-mannered university lecturer to fearless globe-trotting adventurer.

Indiana Jones' hat empowers him with perspective.

> **Perspective is a superpower, enabling you to slay risk and cut it down to size.**

Perspective doesn't eliminate risk; it deals with it effectively and proportionately. Trying to eliminate risk is futile. It's impossible. Risk can only ever be managed.

Perspective tames risk to manageable proportions. Consider, for example, crossing a busy road.

You need to reach the other side. It's a main road, with all manner of vehicles hurtling up and down. Each and every one of those vehicles is moving at speed, each and every one of them could do you an injury. There is potential for a serious accident. This is not an unusual scenario, of course. It's a familiar one that many of us are frequently faced with. Whether you're commuting to work, travelling to school or sourcing a pint of milk, such hazards could be classed as every day. Perspective provides the stillness to calmly assess the right time and place to cross, or not.

Think about it. We are but a step away from potential disaster on a daily basis. Yet it seems we are more proficient at dealing with several tons of hurtling automobile than we are with a creepy crawly. Because we have road sense. In other words, we have perspective. When dealing with the busy road, we have to have perspective. There is literally no room for manoeuvre. When being squeamish about the spider, deep down, we know the consequences of getting it wrong are not life-threatening. Because there is wriggle room, we wriggle.

Most of us implement perspective when we have to – and reasonably successfully at that. Otherwise, we wouldn't last the day. When faced with woolly, indeterminate circumstances (and consequences), however, we rarely feel the urgency. We're less inclined to register what needs to be done and act upon it. This results in apathy, procrastination and a lack of productivity. We need to be more disciplined regarding the need to make informed decisions, rather than cognitively drifting.

Woolly, indeterminate circumstances include:

Resilience 2.0: Embracing Challenge and Change

Preparing for the road ahead

Returning to the road example, perspective is the ability to look both ways and make an informed judgement about the various options and their likely consequences. It doesn't make the road any safer, it makes you safer. The potential for getting squashed still exists, but you have grasped the ability to look left and right, assessing the safest way of proceeding. You have taken the initiative. Indeed, assessing whether or not there is a safe way to proceed. You register the gaps in the traffic, gauge the approximate window of opportunity, weigh your capacity to traverse such a conundrum of time and space, and Bingo! You've successfully crossed over to the other side.

It's worth reiterating perspective doesn't make life any safer, it makes you braver. A lifetime spent playing it safe is really no life at all.

Perspective lubricates the brain, oiling the workings and machinations of cognitive processing and enabling smooth decision making. Without perspective, we're a little clunky. We miss bits, fixate on others and lose sight of the important matters in hand. Perspective does not add anything to our skill set, it just lays all our tools out neatly so that they're readily visible and accessible. Perspective puts our potential within arm's reach, rather than having to rummage in the back of a wardrobe for it. We find ourselves scrabbling around in the dark, not because of the limitations of our abilities, but because they've not yet been sufficiently illuminated.

We've all encountered those seemingly baffling situations, where once someone shines a metaphorical light on the problem, it's no longer a problem. In fact, it seems blindingly obvious! We had the wherewithal to progress all along; it was just a matter of selection. Poor selections – or no selection at all – contaminate our recipes for success. We possess many of the ingredients already, but only tend to scan the ones at the front of the cerebral shelves. Supermarket shelf stackers are regularly required to front-up their produce, ensuring the best-before dates are managed and all stock is clearly visible.

> **The trick to maintaining our personal perspective is to regularly and systematically front-up, showcasing all the tools at our disposal to maintain a balanced perspective all year around.**

The snow globe is one such tool.

Chapter 10

Snow Globe Thinking

Like it or not, we spend a significant proportion of our waking hours on autopilot. It's just easier that way, which appeals to our evolutionary efficiency. Frankly, it would be impossible to sustain the energy levels required to navigate our lives manually 24/7. We all need to switch off or we burn out.

Occasionally, however, our systems are rudely interrupted: overridden when we encounter a little turbulence. Our world is shaken and we come to the startling realisation that we have to act. We are compelled to do something. 'Doing something' is normally marshalled by our reticular activating systems: a way of letting our subconscious mind take the strain. When we encounter something out of the ordinary, we're stirred from our habitual decision-making stupor and begin to take an active interest. Not through choice, but out of necessity.

The need to act requires a decision on how to act. Faced with a scenario in which action is urgently required, the first thing that springs to mind generally fulfils the remit: do 'something… anything', often suffices. At least, in panic mode.

Defaulting

Doing something or nothing is not much of a choice. If you don't like one option, you are left with the other by default, rather than choice. Defaulting is not a strategy for improving life, but one for temporarily prolonging it, until the next time. Improvement is the accumulation of proactive decision making, rather than passively settling for limited (and limiting) alternatives.

Defaulting is what we do, however. It is our default setting.

Defaulting can take various guises:

Defaulting-to-type is primitive reactionary processing, otherwise known as a 'knee-jerk' reaction. It often results in one of the following outcomes:

❖ Doing something, that with hindsight, we wish we hadn't, or
❖ Not doing something that, on reflection, we wish we had.

Neither outcome is beneficial, and both epitomise regret. Defaulting is the origin of regret, impulsively selecting the wrong path when we had the opportunity for better. Or, indeed, not realising the opportunity when we did. We all have regrets at some level, even those who profess not to. Some people don't dwell upon their regrets, but that doesn't mean they wouldn't have acted differently with hindsight.

Resilience 2.0: Embracing Challenge and Change

foreseeing intended outcomes and taking steps towards desirable consequences.

There is a multi-zillion dollar industry invested in controlling your ability to control your ability. Public relations experts have the capacity to step back from a situation, disassociate and evaluate circumstances objectively. Few of us think carefully and make the right decisions in the heat of the moment. The key is to be able to think carefully about when and how to think carefully.

The art of snow globe thinking, therefore, is to refrain from thinking too hard until the worst of the blizzard has blown over and the snow has settled. Only when the neural white-out has cleared do you obtain the clarity and perspective to make an informed decision regarding what to do or not to do. All subsequent decisions are informed decisions, rather than snap judgements made in haste.

If action is called for, the magnitude of response must be proportionate to the conundrum faced. History is littered with disproportionate responses, overreactions that only serve to exacerbate existing problems (and conflicts). Not overreacting requires a similar amount of restraint to 'considered nothing'. Your emotive self will be keen to go over the top, acting impulsively with disproportionate words and actions and often causing unnecessary escalation. If you are part of a group, the voices of reason urging restraint will likely be in the minority. Where there's a pack of people there is also a pack mentality: a real-time echo-chamber that fervently ups the ante. The initial conundrum can very quickly morph into a shared forum for collective social flexing, with little to do with the origins of the dissent. Disagreements are appropriated.

Detach yourself from the noise, the rancour and vitriol of others, for however seemingly well-meaning, it is usually coloured by insecurities and baggage acquired elsewhere, probably from some other time. Your decisions will affect you primarily, and you must be accountable to you. Others are quick to vociferously offer their advice but conspicuously absent should there be any fallout. Respond in a way that you can live with, regardless of consequence, for the foreseeable future. Forever.

In terms of gauging the appropriate magnitude of response, it helps to quantify the predicament you are currently faced with. Otherwise, we fall into a scenario of generalisation that tips reality askew. Everything feels like a 'nightmare' when, in truth, something has merely presented a minor setback. Human beings are quick to catastrophise. We make an inflated off-the-cuff sweeping statement, which quickly becomes absorbed into the parlance of everyday.

> **We are very good at seeing what we say, and it doesn't take long for us to begin inhabiting our own rhetoric and acting accordingly.**

Like a drug, we rapidly become immune to the potency of our language and up the dosage. Before long, we're negativity junkies, irresistibly drawn to making the very worst of a situation, believing our own destructive hype and spinning catastrophe.

We need to take a step back.

My Dad was a statistician. He used numbers to help make sense of the world. I'm not just talking about identifying patterns in the weather, but as a tool for managing mindfulness, positivity and wellbeing. Amongst other things, he used a simple scale to reflect upon his day. Any resulting patterns helped to inform future behaviours and routines that might prove beneficial. At the end of each day, he used a simple scoring system from 1 – 5 to indicate how much he had enjoyed his day. 0 would be the sort of day he wouldn't wish to repeat anytime soon, a 5 would be something special.

When trying to ascertain how much of a problem you are faced with, a simple scoring system helps to cut through the background noise. Scaling is an effective way of getting a grip. Asking yourself on a scale of, for instance, 1 – 10 (with 10 being the direst of consequences), whereabouts your current predicament lies helps to inject some perspective. Tens are thankfully very rare. As are eights and nines. If we're honest, situations with a severity of seven don't crop-up too often, either.

It doesn't matter what scale you use. Some people prefer to keep their scales small (1 to 5) or others prefer larger. The more intervals on the scale, the more flexibility you have for relative comparison with previous events, the more references can be incorporated to shrink the current conundrum down to size. A word of caution: if the scale you select is too extensive, it can lead to indecision and prevarication. Scaling is supposed to be a tool that works for you, rather than a tool that 'works' you!

Scaling works well when called upon, but is most effective if practised frequently as a matter of course. Regularly quantifying your everyday helps to gain and maintain perspective and pre-empt any turbulence. Perspective is useful on both good days and bad and can sometimes provide the right sort of nudge (even when you haven't realised you need one). Segmenting your day in to three distinct zones is also a useful way of gauging your day. Dividing the morning, afternoon and evening into sections helps disassociate a less-than-desirable event from contaminating the entire 24 hours. Just because the morning hasn't quite gone to plan, for instance, doesn't mean it has to impact upon the rest of the day. You can have 'one of those mornings' without it escalating into 'one of those days'.

Once your day has been scaled down to size, it becomes more manageable. But it still requires managing, nevertheless. Even if a particular issue has been shrunk down to size, it can still be a preoccupation and provide distraction. A concerted effort needs to be made to switch your attention, change your focus and move on.

Building a mental bridge can be a powerful metaphor to help put negative concerns behind you. Visualising, overcoming and traversing whatever event is threatening to become a potential barrier, allows you to leave any unwanted baggage behind. We carry all sorts of unnecessary mental baggage with us for years, lugging around memories of unpleasant experiences and tainting our current waking moments. It's time to let them go. You can, and you should, **now**!

Some thoughts are undeniably better left behind, but can be stubborn to shake off, nevertheless. Without making a concerted effort to move on, we become stuck in a toxic spiral of worry, regret and insecurity. Moving on is good and the sooner the better.

Unwanted baggage better left behind:

Resilience 2.0: Embracing Challenge and Change

The key to managing risk is the realisation and acceptance that it is ever present. There is no escaping it. Your acknowledgement of potential danger keeps you safe. Identifying possible hazards allows you to safely negotiate them. Remaining blissfully unaware puts you at even more risk, only you don't realise it. Some people stick their heads in the sand hoping to progress through life blissfully ignorant, yet this is often a short-lived strategy that leads to a rude awakening. Or at least, a somewhat underwhelming existence, as umpteen positive opportunities are missed.

> **Managing risk means managing ourselves. We possess the tools and wherewithal to navigate 100% of the situations we encounter to the best of our ability.**

That doesn't mean we can avoid every negative outcome, just that we can make the best of a good or bad situation. Armed with that realisation, it's possible to move forwards in life with less trepidation about what the future may or may not hold. Because you can genuinely make the very best of it, whatever it might be, if you learn to put your mind to it.

Bad stuff happens, of course. Many of those things are entirely out of your control. By realising and accepting you can only focus upon and respond to events within the realms of your sphere of influence, we can let the other stuff go. Ultimately, a catastrophe may or may not be avoided, but managing circumstances to the best of your ability stops you from catastrophising. In some situations, what will be will be. In the meantime, you might as well make the most of it.

Things that might be worth the risk:

Chapter 11

Retention

Most people entertain the notion of change – to a point. Retention is that point. It's the point at which you've tried, tried and tried again, but to no avail. Good intentions end with a lack of retention, when really, it should be just the beginning.

We all start off with good intentions. Joining a gym, enrolling in a night class, buying a new set of pans: the sentiment is admirable. We're prepared to put our money where our mouth is. When we commit to doing something, we're genuinely all in. We mean it.

All in commitment comes in different forms and guises:

None of these commitments is undertaken lightly. Many require a great deal of courage. When we really put our minds to something, when we genuinely decide 'enough is enough', it's surprising what we're capable of.

Painful memories

It's also quite surprising what we're **not** capable of. Think back to an occasion when you've wholeheartedly thrown yourself into a new venture, only for it to peter out into an expensive about turn. Indeed, we try not to think of such occasions, because the failings can feel embarrassing, painful, even. We don't like to be reminded of a particular 'phase' that ended ignominiously. To compound the embarrassment, others might find it a source of amusement and pour scorn on our lacklustre attempts. What were we thinking of, after all? We should know our place and not get ideas above our station.

Painful memories curtail any future attempt at learning, growth and betterment. Because we failed last time, and are still smarting, we want to avoid repeating the humiliation. We suspect the very same people who ridiculed our efforts previously will redouble their efforts this time. Or at least, that's how it feels, anyway. We don't learn from our mistakes because we try to do everything possible to bury and ignore them. In a world of social media fiction, where everyone else is apparently living the dream, the currency of a polished highlights reel is the one that seems to count. The true story, however, is not the airbrushed popular one of overnight success, where anyone can make it by uploading a clip on to YouTube the night before. Yet anything falling short of the (albeit impossible) online idyll is relegated to the recycle bin.

> **People are embarrassed of falling short when they should be proud of falling; if you never let go, you'll never have the chance to fly.**

Without learning from your mistakes, there simply is no learning. Success without endeavour is merely good fortune. Good fortune runs out sooner or later, however lucky you are. In terms of incremental improvement, retention is central to making successful progress through the conscious competence stage. You can't measure your ability until you've given your skills every chance to develop.

A good idea doesn't suddenly become a bad idea. The aspiration remains just as valid. Getting fit, starting a new business, studying for a PhD… all remain noble ambitions, even if you run out of ambition. We give things up as a bad idea when they're actually a very good idea, primarily because they've not progressed beyond the idea stage. Lack of traction doesn't necessarily make the idea a bad one. The more important consideration is what terminated the pursuit? What dulled the fire and snuffed out the flames? Ambition once burned brightly, after all, before it petered out.

'Petering out' suggests something of an embarrassing retreat, going out with a whimper. It implies quietly slinking away in defeat, with a proverbial tail between the legs, chastened by an unsuccessful foray into personal improvement. 'Petering' is not giving up, however. It's not indicative of flawed character, lack of moral fibre or backbone. Quite the opposite.

The truth? When the going gets tough, the majority of us don't get going. We're unavoidably human, and it's made evolutionary sense for us to cut our losses. Survival requires a delicate balancing act between effort expended and the pursuit of that which replenishes effort, thus creating an ultimatum: stick or twist? Life has always revolved around this moment of reckoning. There is a point of no return and the point that pays a return. The consequences of misjudging the former are arguably more serious than the latter. Giving up – cutting our losses – means we live to fight another day. Going quietly gives you the option of building back stronger. Petering out is a tactical retreat.

The point at which stick-becomes-twist is pivotal to our capacity to retain – to continue pursuing our good intentions. Some 99% of us fall significantly short. We get nowhere near fulfilling our potential and instead make a conservatively premature about-face.

We all 'think' we've reached the point where enough is enough. The end of your tether is not actually the end of your tether, however. Your tether is actually more of a retractable dog lead, and with a bit of encouragement, there's plenty more to be coaxed out.

Some typical fake tether endings:

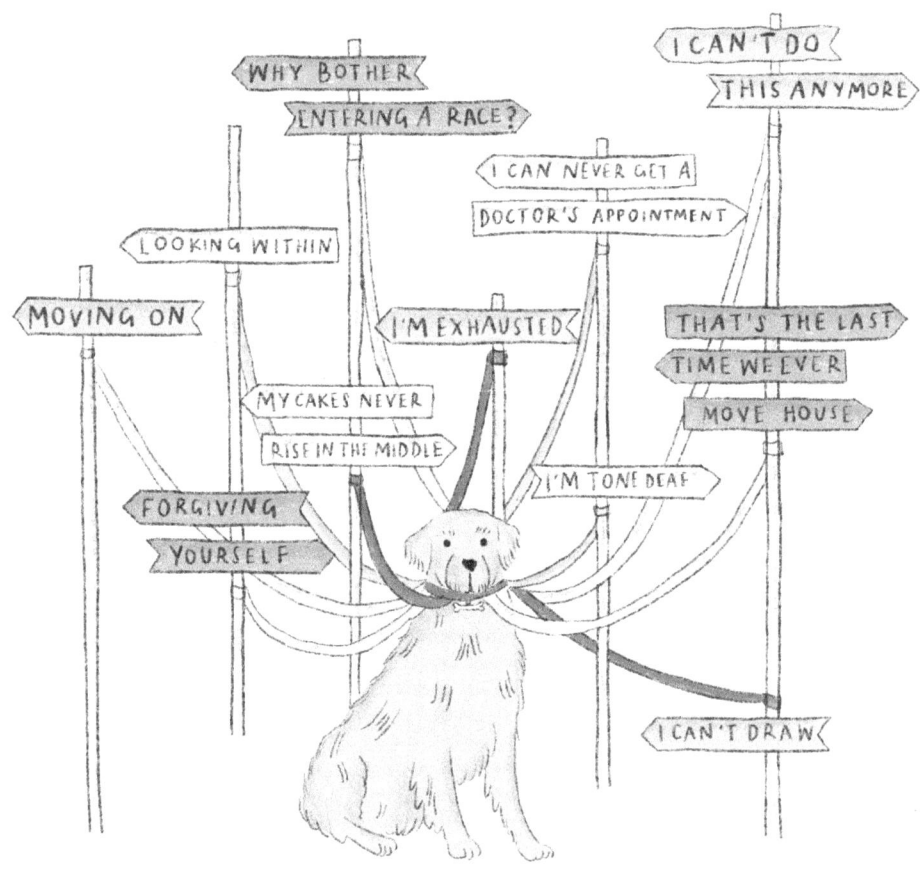

Resilience 2.0: Embracing Challenge and Change

Happy endings

Tethered endings are not always clearly evident; they sneakily creep up on you. The starts just get further and further apart, perpetually delayed until you no longer initiate anything. Your start has inadvertently stopped and you've terminated by default. Consider the last time your New Year's resolution became less resolute. At some point you stopped doing what you set out to do, but I'm guessing the actual point might be quite hazy? Endings are usually a subtle lapse. They gradually creep up on you a bit like old age: you know it's happened but it's difficult to say quite when.

Establishing good habits is about implementing good practice at regular intervals throughout the course of your day/week/month, depending upon the nature of your undertaking. You're creating periodical reference points for your attention, to avoid subconscious wanderings into other realms of interest. Your attention is a finite resource. Retention requires your focus and concentration, which requires you to focus and concentrate. That might sound blindingly obvious, but many people indulge in habits without sufficient conscious investment, resulting in little or no benefit.

Consider reading a page of a book. How often have you read an entire segment only to realise you have absolutely no comprehension of its content? You've gone through the motions of decoding without any recollection or understanding of the text. There is a disconnect between your physical machinations and capacity to retain meaning. Your mind has wandered even if your body remained present. Cognitive absenteeism is behind some of your most unproductive days. Alternatively, some days you might feel as though you've achieved nothing, yet you've actually been reasonably productive. You've addressed tasks that weren't on your linear 'to-do' list at the beginning of the day. Even though you may not have ticked-off any of the planned tasks, you've 'freestyled' and been productive, nevertheless. On other days, nothing gets done because you can't focus. Or rather, your focus has been elsewhere: booking a summer holiday, a dispute with your neighbour or maybe what you're having for tea that night.

> **Success depends upon the ability to keep your head in the game. When something's amiss, it's worth considering that it might actually be you.**

Let's consider 'revision' for a moment. It's an open-ended task. Arguably, there is always more that can be done. The vagaries of completion make it challenging to sustain focus. Completion is the ultimate attention reference point. When the end is nowhere in sight – and you wouldn't even know what it looked like if it was – remaining focused is nigh on impossible. Outwardly, we busy ourselves with the chattels and rituals of retention. Organising flashcards, procuring different coloured pens, and shuffling ring-binders can occupy us for hours. All of which are a distraction from the primary purpose of revision. Outwardly, we've worked. Inwardly, we've gone AWOL.

Pursuing anything successfully requires regular and identifiable 'endings' to quantify improvement. An ending works as both a 'push' and a 'pull' factor in maintaining and supplementing your reserves of attention. Having a 'fixed' point to aim for is often all that's required to stay on course. Consider learning to swim. There is a reason why fledgling swimmers are awarded 10m and 25m badges and so on. Such benchmarks signify the end of a struggle (at least for the time being) which works as a powerful incentive. Without the finality provided by a distance marker, 18, 19 or 20 meters might be the perceived limit. The finish line pulls you through the last hard yards. If you see the finish line, the end is in sight.

The finish line also pushes you to go further. Anyone who has successfully completed a marathon will likely have experienced feelings of 'never again!' It's amazing how quickly the pain and discomfort dissolve, however, to be replaced by thoughts of the next adventure.

Recent success gives licence to dream what might now be possible. What might be next. It propels you forward.

Retention is built upon finish lines and finish lines accumulate retention. They form the steps of your staircase. The key is to establish sufficient 'finishing lines' to charter your daily progress. The appropriate amount, nature and extent of finish lines vary from person to person, and also from day to day. They are also, of course, dependent upon the nature of the tasks involved. Perhaps the most important factor to start with, however, is your starting point.

Clearly, the starting point for a seasoned 10k runner aspiring to complete her first marathon, is very different to someone recovering from a stroke who shares the same ambition. The starting point for an aspiring postgraduate keen to attend medical school is very different to a student struggling with formal academia. Starting points are relevant but they are not defining. Regardless of the starting point, the end is in the same place. It is a fixed target – 26.2 miles is always going to be 26.2 miles – no longer, no shorter. A doctorate is a doctorate; the same criteria apply. The fulfilment of a dream isn't any further away for you than the next person, it's just a matter of time. The horizon remains constant, regardless of where you are. We are all on different points on our individual roads. The road finishes in the same place for all of us, even if our starts are staggered.

Creating personal primers

Personally, I require several 'finish lines' to help navigate my daily routines. What's interesting, is that many of these arguably have no explicit bearing upon a particular goal. Indirectly, however, they are invaluable. They are primers. Priming ensures I am in the correct physical and mental state to fully focus and apply myself. The tasks themselves may sound fairly innocuous yet provide a vehicle for honing my emotional readiness. If I don't do what I have to do, what I really have to do doesn't get done.

Such abstraction is something I've learned to embrace. For years, I worried the various routines and rituals were just prevarication, but I've gradually learnt to understand them as being the exact opposite. They are essential ingredients integral to generating a state of flow, the state when I am undeniably most focused, creative, productive and – dare I say – inspired. A ten-minute period immersed in a 'flow' state is far more productive than a whole day of synthetic labouring.

It takes a brave person to prioritise priming, as from the outside it can seem unnecessarily self-indulgent. A short-sighted boss values apparent industry over consideration. This is an all too common workplace scenario, often resulting in the wrong people being rewarded for doing the wrong thing. The right people are often chastised for their lack of visible productivity, overshadowed by others loudly signalling their faux contribution and worth.

It pays to have the courage of your convictions, however, and devote dedicated time and space to laying the foundations required for bringing your best. Proceeding in any other fashion is inauthentic and ultimately garners resentment, unfulfillment and dissatisfaction. Everyone should learn to dance to their own personal beat. This requires listening carefully to yourself, and heeding your own unique individual wants, needs, rhythms and requirements.

Priming tasks integral to writing this book include:

* Eating two apples a day (probably Braeburn)
* Cutting the apples into small segments (they taste nicer that way)
* Going for a run every day. Ensuring I complete the requisite distance/intensity. If there is a choice between two routes, I must take the more challenging option
* Giving the dog some fuss and attention
* Ensuring all software updates are completed
* Taking a zinc tablet supplement

* Challenging myself to complete Wordle
* Emptying the dishwasher
* Completing the Rubik's cube at least once in a day
* A 60-minute gym workout, including core exercises and (most importantly) stretching
* Eating two oranges
* Reading. Preferably fiction
* Connecting with family.

Not all tasks have to be completed every day, but each somehow transports me towards a place of productivity. Retention is the relentless pursuit of your endeavour, which requires stamina. Stamina is a core ingredient of momentum. Every single action that primes your capacity to keep moving forward, to stay in the game, to remain focused and spurn disillusionment, is a worthwhile pursuit. You are investing in you. You complete the marathon; you write the book and you shed three stone. Anything that promotes a better version of you, is worth investing in. Remember, cultivating resilience is about the whole you.

Priming may seem to some a little obsessive and compulsive. It is. Prioritising the behaviours and rituals necessary to succeed requires a single-minded determination. If you don't care enough, you'll soon lose traction. Caring too much can be self-destructive. It's a balancing act that needs to be got just right. Only you can find your equilibrium.

Chapter 12

The End of the Road

We have not reached the end of the section dedicated to retention, but we have reached the 'end of the road'. This bit deserves a whole chapter to itself because all too often it's the graveyard of dreams.

The 'end of the road' describes that seemingly insurmountable obstacle that will undoubtedly present: an impossible barrier to the continued pursuit of that which you've hitherto set about. Overcoming it will be a sure test of your resilience upgrade.

Improvement is essentially acquisition: endeavouring to develop the knowledge, skills, or attributes that, for whatever reason, have so far alluded you. Lack of experience means lack of acquisition.

We have a tendency to confuse our lack of experience with a lack of application and ability. Ability is absolutely not limitless. Despite what you may have read, it's simply not true to say that you can be anyone you want to be, just so long as you put your mind to it. I will never win a gold medal for the 100m sprint in the Olympics: I'm too old, too slow and too late. Physiologically, I don't have the tools (and have never had the tools) to compete with someone who is stuffed with fast-twitch muscle fibres and eminently more biologically suited to sprinting. That said, there's nothing stopping me from running as fast as I possibly can, if I really put my mind to it. The only thing that is stopping me is me. I can achieve my gold medal.

When enough isn't enough

We are the biggest barrier to fulfilling our potential – not that seemingly insurmountable obstacle at the end of the road. The true extent of our ability is rarely realised because we emotionally bale out. We're okay when the going gets tough. When the going gets *really*

Resilience 2.0: Embracing Challenge and Change

tough, however, most of us decide that enough is enough and self-preservation kicks in. Often, rather than acknowledge 'giving up' we subconsciously choose an alternative path or interest, one that we convince ourselves is actually a better idea or more fruitful endeavour. We displace our focus and effectively give in by stealth.

The honest truth is that we don't fully commit our minds to it. We put our mind to something else, which is not quite the same. Genuinely putting your mind to it requires staying on track, remaining on target, and stubbornly refusing to deviate from your original goal. Deviating is the easy option in the short term, but it's a perennial sidestep. Sidestepping means you are forever doomed to traverse goals without ever fulfilling potential.

Putting your mind to it is where application comes in, which is what this book is all about. Receptivity requires us to be up for a challenge, remember, and risk requires the bravery to go for it. Retention is all about having the mental fortitude to stick with it. Human beings have enormous capacity to persevere through thick and thin, good times and bad, through the ups and the downs. Having endured all of that, then what a waste it would be to throw in the towel.

But throw in the towel, we do.

It is a bit like reaching Camp 3 of Mount Everest only to give up because the summit remains shrouded in cloud. You might not be able to see the summit, but that doesn't diminish how far you've come. Only by looking back can you truly measure your progress, yet we are fixated with 'forward' motion. Just because you are not there yet doesn't mean you haven't come an awfully long way. Looking back at your achievements is a powerful tool for reinvigorating your enthusiasm. The 'priming finish lines' we have discussed are useful benchmarks for acknowledging the progress made so far.

Despite all of this, we still reach a point of realisation that enough is enough. We've reached the end of our limits and can do know more. We've given it our best shot and have nothing left to give.

That's how it feels, anyway.

Honestly?

> **When it feels like you've reached the end of the road, believe me, you haven't. There is more to you than you think.**

Moving past, what can more accurately be described as a temporary roadblock, is what separates the great from the good. That doesn't mean it is easy, of course – far from it. It is very, very hard. But it is possible, nevertheless. You are stronger and more capable than you think you are. Possibility is key when slaying the dragon of doubt.

To push the realms of possibility and banish the self-doubts that curtail us, conversation is vital. The right words at the right time initiate the right actions to help us stay the course. Positive self-talk isn't delusional, it's manifest. Articulating just how we're going to get our head around an obstacle, is the process that creates the circumnavigation. You've got to be inwardly active, constantly agitating and seeking answers to progress. Alternatively, a passive mind creates a vacuum, which is soon filled by all manner of distractions causing deviation from your ultimate goal.

Deviation is the enemy of productivity. By convincing ourselves we've got something else to do, we subconsciously create licence to give up on our original course. It pays to remind ourselves of what we're doing and why we're doing it, before a supposedly 'better' idea comes along. Better ideas are always better just so long as they remain ideas. The reality is usually just as challenging as your current one, which

Resilience 2.0: Embracing Challenge and Change

you have already made significant inroads towards. Changing tack actually means starting again, which isn't progression. Changing tack is disengaging from the original process of change.

Internal dialogue is what helps you stay the course until a glimmer of a breakthrough presents: that wonderful moment when you realise the dream is still alive. If not a way ahead, then a signpost suggesting there might be. You are not out of ideas. Internal dialogue helps to reveal fresh options. There are always alternatives.

Having a conversation with yourself should be a regular feature of your day. It's not madness – quite the opposite. Conversations can directly relate to your chosen goal, the activities required to prime your productivity, and those benchmark 'finish lines'.

Potential topics for internal dialogue:

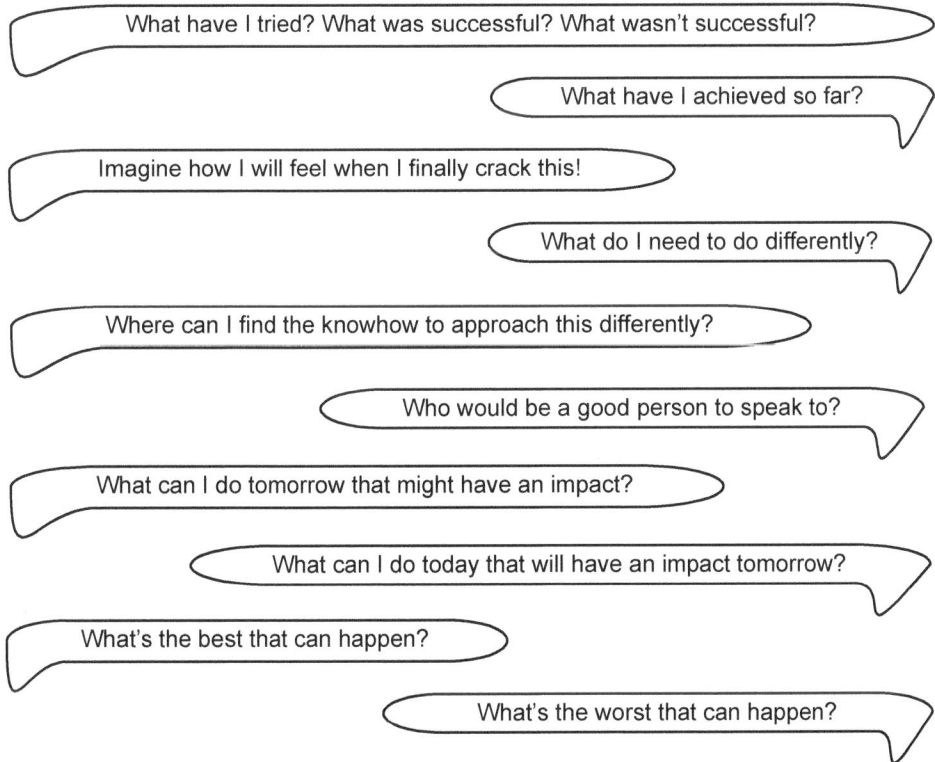

What have I tried? What was successful? What wasn't successful?

What have I achieved so far?

Imagine how I will feel when I finally crack this!

What do I need to do differently?

Where can I find the knowhow to approach this differently?

Who would be a good person to speak to?

What can I do tomorrow that might have an impact?

What can I do today that will have an impact tomorrow?

What's the best that can happen?

What's the worst that can happen?

There will be some prompts that prove particularly effective for you. Asking questions, asking something, anything, is the best way of finding out what they might be. You cannot not respond.

Ultimately, to push on through, you must somehow summon the inner strength, courage and fortitude to force yourself to continue. When those inner reserves have been tapped once, they become easier to access and are transferable to other areas of your life. Simply knowing you've got what it takes does wonders for facing up to very different yet equally challenging situations. Essentially, you don't sweat the small stuff. You know from experience you're made of the right stuff.

Under par?

Hitting a golf ball into a hole is a blissfully simple concept for a game. The fewer goes it takes, the more successful you are. The game is a competition of economy, greater skill results in more efficiency. Success is doing less rather than more.

Consider putting a golf ball into a cup as a metaphor for progress and improvement. The distance is about 10 feet, and you can make as many attempts as you wish. The task seems straightforward enough; the success criteria is clear, and you have the resources required at your disposal. Chances are, you won't succeed at the first attempt, or even the second. After a variable number of attempts, you might still be some way off and beginning to lose interest. This is when things become a little murky. Somewhere in our psyche, success can become confused. Putting the ball in the cup could well become the overriding requirement, justifying whatever means necessary in doing so. Should no one else be present to bear witness, the cup can be moved slightly closer, and then maybe a little closer still. The nature of the task has remained the same, after all. What harm can it do? After foreshortening several times, you successfully put the ball into the cup and have achieved your goal.

Unfortunately, success has been achieved but at the expense of any genuinely meaningful progress. Repeating the feat remains something of a lottery, particularly if recalibrating the original distance. Whilst, arguably, we've succeeded, we have not benefitted from a learning opportunity. Instead, we have foregone the opportunity of useful feedback in our haste to secure a modicum of success – however hollow. A greater number of considered repetitions would have increased our level of skill, as we become 'better' at failing before transitioning to success. Genuine improvement requires a task being repeated incrementally, alternatively and, eventually, successfully.

Mitigating failure at the earliest possible opportunity is a common human trait. We are predisposed to taking shortcuts, despite convincing ourselves otherwise.

We are great pretenders, selective in both attitudes and application.

There is no fast-track on the road to success, however. The fastest way is the authentic way. Remaining vigilant of the tendency to fabricate success helps counter our subliminal subterfuge. We know when we're falling short and should not pretend otherwise.

The hard yards are usually the most valuable yards. Withstanding the opposite of an 'easy' option cultivates a robust resilient mindset, helping develop neurostamina and sustaining retention. Our ability to resist the path of least resistance can be conditioned over time.

Practices for cultivating every-day retention include:

- Going a little further on your morning run than planned
- Reading your son a bedtime story when you have work to do
- Regularly checking on a vulnerable neighbour
- Saving the chocolate for later

* Walking rather than taking the bus
* Hanging the washing on the line rather than using the tumble dryer
* Completing a crossword
* Preparing a packed lunch the 'night before'
* Waiting for the green light to cross the road.

Encountering setbacks can threaten to scupper our retention. Setbacks come in all shapes and sizes, both major and minor. It can be quite hard to distinguish their magnitude, because every setback can seem like a big deal when you are in the thick of it. Small setbacks don't feel small and big setbacks are catastrophic. We crave success, ideally without incident.

Damage celebration

We know by now, however, that the road to success is rarely a smooth one. It's full of potholes and littered with discarded dreams. When it all feels a little off-putting, consider the Japanese practice of *Kintsugi*.

Kintsugi might at first seem like a damage-limitation exercise, but it's actually far from it, indeed quite the opposite. It's an exercise in damage celebration.

Breakfast time is not supposed to be a time for breakages, but many a cereal bowl has met its demise through a combination of bleary-eyed handling and running late. Suffice to say, we've all suffered our fair share of spillages. Such mishaps are typically punctuated by decidedly liberal language and a flourish of the dustpan and brush. The evidence is quickly disposed of, and normal service is resumed.

Kintsugi is not normal service. Rather than an unfortunate incident best forgotten, it's valued as an opportunity for growth and development. Rather than destruction, the focus is upon reassimilation: in essence, building back better. The constituent pieces are carefully gathered and put safely aside for such a time as they can be given due consideration.

A bit like a three-dimensional jigsaw, *Kintsugi* extols the value of investing the time and effort in to reassembling the broken item. The process is not just cathartic, but regenerative: creating something that did not previously exist. Each piece of the damaged item is carefully glued back together with the utmost care. The aim is not to make it 'as good as new,' however, but even better. To add value and worth by means of the meticulous investment of care and concentration. Rather than using an invisible adhesive in attempting to mask the damage, a special mixture of gold paint and resin is used to deliberately draw attention to any imperfections. The piece is to be celebrated. It is now deemed to be more valuable by dint of the considerable additional care and attention it has received. It is 'flawsome'.

Kintsugi is a metaphor for growth. Progress is never, ever linear. Things rarely go to plan, even with the best-laid plans. There's an old saying that 'failing to prepare is preparing to fail'. I'd suggest that preparing for failure is true preparation, however. Failure and success are inextricably linked. The nature of all growth is endeavouring to acquire. It's simply not possible to go from ignorance to excellence without a learning curve. Understanding that the learning curve is riddled with anomalies is steeling yourself for the task in question.

Success is all about our relationship with failure.

> **The better we fail the more likely we are to succeed.**

Kintsugi shows the value of embracing adversity. The trials and tribulations we experience in any endeavour are an inescapable integral part of the challenge. Without challenge, there is no endeavour. Without endeavour, there is no growth. We aspire because we desire that which we do not have. The vacuum between aspiring and acquiring is filled with failure and success. Failure and success are inseparable, one defines the other. Without failure you can not appreciate success. The possibility of success brings the possibility of failure. Only by tackling obstacles do we develop the fortitude to overcome them.

Every time you strive for improvement, your response is unique. Your personalised journey of learning is particular to your own thoughts, experiences, attributes and application. Engaging with improvement creates scope for developing greater diversity, broadening your horizons and making you even more unique. Our differences are the very qualities that define our identity. By embracing opportunities to further explore and express our unique individuality, we grow.

Failure…

Viewing failure differently is essential for retention, and it's important to deal with it positively. Failure should be a driving force which helps motivate you to get out of bed in the morning. Not being able to do something is often a greater motivator than being able to do it. After completing your first marathon, for instance, it can subsequently feel harder to get up and running in the morning. That itch has been scratched. Success can feel empty, or at least short-lived. Lack of success is a rich source to mine. The things we can't do channel our energies and resources into a driving force. Without that drive there would be stagnation. We need to fail to feel alive.

Significant failures might or might not include:

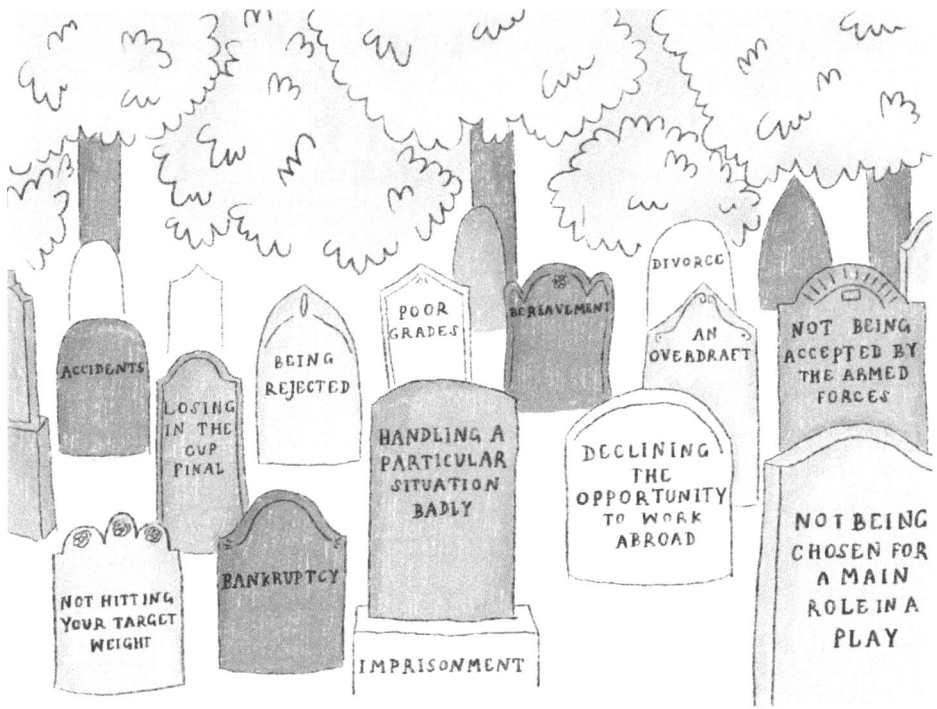

Culture

Most of us wouldn't choose any of the failures illustrated above, but they can prove to be valuable transformative opportunities, nevertheless. They might be easier to acknowledge in hindsight, but with some degree of foresight can kindle a sense of optimism. Foresight is not always easily accessible, and can require some careful soul-searching, especially when it's hard to see past the end of the day.

Of the five stages of cultivating resilience, retention is perhaps the most time-consuming. In terms of incremental improvement, conscious competence is the prevailing sentiment. As such, we are very aware of our questionable rate of progress, making it feel more cumbersome than it actually is. We might see little reward for extended periods of endeavour and application. Retention is typically where growth stalls, as we grapple with seemingly insurmountable obstacles. Rest assured, however, that your ability is slowly growing like bacterial culture in your potential petri dish. You have to let nature take its course once the right conditions for growth have been crafted. All you can do is work on the factors that are within your control and wait for your mind and body to explore their own conclusions. This should be a liberating thought: one that allows you to look upon yourself more kindly and acknowledge the strides taken thus far.

We are very good at doing ourselves down, when talking ourselves up is actually what's required. Some research a few years back suggested we give far greater weighting to negative thoughts than positive. This resonates with my personal experience. Negative thoughts stick. Positive thoughts are fleeting in comparison. Anyone who has experienced some sort of professional appraisal likely remembers the 'points for improvement' more than what's deemed to be 'going well'. Similarly, if you've ever been dumped before, the 'it's not you it's me' platitudes do little to numb the sense of rejection. Negativity has armour-piercing casing. Positivity is caked with blancmange and slips through our fingers.

When it comes to accepting praise, it seems our defences are already fully formed – maybe even 'overdeveloped'. We're so used to cultivating a 'thick skin' in preparation for mitigating the possibility of criticism,

Resilience 2.0: Embracing Challenge and Change

that it often takes us unawares and feels destabilising. Rather than just accepting a compliment, we brush it off. We're big on belittling ourselves. We routinely dismiss feedback, possibly in the hope that if/when bad news should come along, it may somehow be easier to ignore.

In terms of retention, it pays to remember how far you've come. Rather than spending a lifetime attempting to develop an impregnable outer shell, making us impervious to criticism, failure or just about anything unwarranted, we must think… Gore-Tex.

Breathe

> Thinking 'Gore-Tex' is probably easier than thinking 'polytetrafluoroethylene;' the expanded material discovered in a happy accident by a father-and-son development team in the late sixties. Gore and Gore Junior created a waterproof, windproof, breathable material that has since been used in a whole host of applications, most notably sportswear.
>
> Gore-Tex is not a thick skin. It's relatively lightweight and allows a range of conditions to be managed, experienced, embraced and enjoyed. It's a multi-purpose material, which allows humans to be more human. It's not a barrier, yet somehow alleviates the worst the elements can throw at you.

Our own skin should be more Gore-Tex. Rather than trying to insulate ourselves from feedback, we should instead be processing information and associated emotions and letting them pass through. The negative doesn't need to saturate us; we can let the learning permeate without being weighed down and hindered. Our minds and bodies can exist in harmony across the whole spectrum of feedback, once we realise that it's not intended to be directed towards us, but instead channelled through. Learning is a process, and we are the vehicles for processing.

Whatever form raw feedback arrives in does not in itself provide value. It's how we choose to harness, interpret and utilise it. Feedback is processed and refined as befits our own individual, unique set of circumstances, rather than blindly and unconditionally accepted. There is no one better placed to understand the inner working and intricacies of you than you. You – and only you – possess the personal insight to justify 'taking or leaving it' and the extent to which you do either. It's not the feedback that is valuable 'per se', but how you choose to act upon it. Upgrading resilience requires filtering unique to you.

> **Recognising that all feedback is neural nutrition allows you to master your emotions. Neither fearful of criticism or beholden to external praise, you can select the pieces deemed to be constructive, helpful and worthwhile.**

This detached approach also enables us to separate the criticism (constructive or not) from the criticiser. The personality of the person delivering the information (and our relationship with) can often overshadow any potential benefits to be taken. Others are entitled to their opinion, but you are more entitled to your opinion when it concerns you! You are best placed to decide what may or may not be in your best interests, and what action (if any) should be taken.

A good talking to

Key to retention is sifting through the quagmire of direct and indirect feedback we receive every day, not least from ourselves. A productive internal dialogue shepherds, censors, dissects and assimilates information before we take it to heart. How we feel about our progress informs our approach to continuing the journey we're on. We need to have a word with ourselves on a regular basis. This is not just good practice for monitoring progress, but also for maintaining positive mental health and well being. We all have conflicting voices in our heads vying for our attention – our very own cast of Mr Men and Little Misses, if you like.

Collectively they're known as our internal dialogue and some are more likely to aggressively elbow their way to the forefront of minds than others. Some of the characters are significantly more vocal and domineering than others – usually the critical naysayers and doom-mongers urging you to quit now. These are the little blighters that need firmly and politely putting in their place. There does not need to be any drama; quietly and calmly shut them down once they start piping up, and before they get a foothold in to your psyche.

We give way too much time and energy to entertaining our personal destructive tendencies. Instead, learn to read the signs and just say 'no' at the first indication. Don't go there in the first place.

We're always aware when something occupies too much head space, yet it doesn't stop us from authorising it. We continue to poke the beehive despite repeatedly being stung. Forget it. Don't go there. You don't have to dwell unnecessarily. Martyrdom is not helpful. Give yourself the same calm reassurance you would your five-year-old son or daughter. Take your own advice. You know the right answers, just listen to them. Don't suffer for your art unnecessarily. In fact, don't suffer at all, or at least without good reason. If you're going about the right sort of business in the right sort of way, you should take more from it than it takes from you. Timely advice. Talking of which…

Timely reminder

Projecting the time scale involved for an undertaking is often the enemy of retention. We typically underestimate or overestimate. The prospect of something taking too long tests our endurance to breaking point, whilst completing ahead of schedule leaves us in limbo, questioning the quality of our application. We wonder if we have taken unlicensed short cuts and start overthinking our practice.

Time is an artificial construct. We create minutes and seconds and months and years to try to provide some sort of order and structure.

I'm not suggesting it's a bad idea, just that it's not always timely or in order. On the plus side, you know where to be at a certain time. On the negative side, you don't always use that time productively. Measuring chunks of time expended doesn't always equate to creating value. We can achieve a lot in a relatively short space of time, and the complete opposite is also true. It's best to forget about how long something is taking, because this tends to be a distraction from focusing upon the nature of the task itself. Far better to concentrate on that which demands attention for as long as feels appropriate. The ticking of the clock is no judge of your effectiveness. Your effectiveness is the measure of your effectiveness. Your productivity is the measure of your productivity. You are the measure of you.

It sometimes feels like you can live a whole day before breakfast, which I'd like to think is a good thing. Catch the day right, squeeze in a run, pop the washing on the line and work on a side hustle or two, and you can bask in the rest of the day knowing you've already smashed it. Everything feels like a bonus when you've used your time wisely (rather than being hamstrung by a time fixation). Your day can be as long or as short as you want it to be. Feel free to sneak in an extra hour whenever you see fit.

Sometimes the end – achieving our desired goal or outcome – seems just too far away. Retention is as much about 'beginnings' and 'middles' as 'ends', however. Sticking at it requires paying attention to the daily detail, the habits and practices woven into the fabric of our daily routines. The positive action that is required now. Change is something that happens right now. It does not need waiting for. Far from being distant and faraway, it's ever-present.

Look after today and tomorrow will take care of itself. Do what is required of you today and do exactly the same tomorrow and the day after and the day after, and so on. That's not repetition, that's just living: being mindful of a succession of current moments. Living in any other moment is a waste. Life is a series of 'nows' and you can manage right now. If you can manage this 'now', you can manage the next and then the next. You can tame this moment and manipulate it at will.

> **Wearing *this* moment well is the only thing that is ever required of you.**

Focusing upon stringing the 'nows' together allows the past and the future to take care of themselves. Do not be burdened by distant predictions. You can only get there by dealing with the here and now.

Retention is actually just the beginning: the art of beginning afresh every single day. It's the point where the basics begin to come together and create a baseline degree of competency. Until now your efforts have been front-loaded; considerable investment has seemingly yielded little value. Unseen, however, is the dormant potential you've been cultivating. Retention gradually nurtures this potential into the open. You are beginning to bloom.

Retention signals a rudimentary grasp of the basics. On the outside there may be nothing particularly impressive about the level of competence you've developed. On the outside, that is. On the inside, there are big changes afoot. You've put in the hard yardage. Be kind to yourself and acknowledge just how far you've come. You deserve it.

A word about haircuts. Or rather, not having hair cut. Most of us have tried 'growing' our hair at some point. Truthfully, long hair suits some people. Others, it most definitely does not.

As we all know, cultivating lovely long locks requires navigating a particularly challenging phase commonly known as 'the in-between stage'. This is the stage when your hair looks neither here nor there, screaming 'neglect'. Parents will describe you as looking 'unkempt', lovers will wonder what attracted them to you in the first place, and people in the street start giving you a noticeably wider berth. However you style your hair, there just isn't a good look during the in-between stage.

For every person who has succeeded in achieving official 'long hair' status, there are probably a dozen who fall by the wayside. Upon reaching the in-between stage, your appearance takes a turn for the worst. The draw of the scissors is strong, as you ponder a rapid return to your previous style. Maybe the long grass isn't always greener, after all?

Navigating the in-between stage is painful. You have to look at yourself differently every single day, and it takes some adjustment. The sight of you can actually feel uncomfortable, and your hair can prove an annoyance and an irritation. It takes a long time. Growing your hair over your ears is follicular purgatory. You couldn't make yourself look any worse if you tried. In so many ways, it makes sense to give up and revert to the short-haired version of you. Nobody will comment, you won't get noticed, people will stop avoiding you and you can pretend it never happened. Go back to the way things were. People won't think any less of you.

You won't think any more of you, however. In fact, you may well feel decidedly let down. You wanted to try long hair, after all. You might look really good with long hair, and now you're never going to know. Ever! You'll carry on wondering, constantly thinking 'what if?' If only you'd stuck with it, it would be long enough to tie back by now. If only…

Life – and, in particular, retention – is the art of navigating the in-between stage. It takes time. How much, is not an exact science, but as a general rule of thumb, a minimum of ten times longer than you anticipated. Patience and commitment are what's required in equal plentiful helpings. The motivation to start should be sufficient

Resilience 2.0: Embracing Challenge and Change

and followed the examples of umpteen others. Growth has been based upon copying what has worked well for those that have gone before you. Mining external experience is a valuable tool and proves particularly helpful when tackling the initial gradient of a steep learning curve. It helps to overcome the inertia of ignorance.

Following the example of others helps bring you up to speed and grasp a basic understanding. It will likely do so relatively speedily, as you absorb the quick wins of others whilst avoiding their pitfalls. Learning from mentors, listening to advice and generally taking heed of those who have 'been there and done that' is invaluable.

Up to a point.

A bit like a bespoke suit, one experience doesn't fit all – perfectly, at least.

> **If your true potential is to be explored, at some point you have to be prepared to go it alone.**

Ultimately, peak performance is not a team game. That doesn't mean that a team cannot perform to a level of collective excellence, of course, just that, to reach those heady heights, the individuals who make up the constituent parts must individually be firing on all cylinders. You are best placed to configure your best.

Taking responsibility doesn't require you to discard the learning and good practice acquired thus far. It's not about throwing out the baby with the bathwater. It is, however, about encouraging you to be your very own trailblazer, following in your own footsteps. Whatever you need to do, whatever practices you need to cultivate and habits that need to be instilled to fulfil your potential, there's a point from which only you can fathom. Up until now, your experience is akin to acquiring the pieces of a jigsaw. The trick now is to arrange them into a new configuration, a unique self-portrait of personal improvement and refinement. Your competence has likely reached a level of unconscious sophistication, presenting new skills to draw upon and experiment with. However, now might be the time to let go…

Unlearning

They say old habits die hard but new ones die harder. Your progress thus far has been centred around the stuff that's helped bring you up to speed. True potential is another gear, however. To access your top gear may require a spot of unlearning: letting go of what's got you this far. I call this the 'stabiliser effect'.

If you can ride a bike, there's a strong possibility your learning was aided by the use of stabilisers: an additional set of wheels to help keep you upright. No doubt they were helpful, as you ultimately succeeded. The stabilisers stopped you from falling off for long enough to gain your balance, developing confidence in doing so.

Only stabilisers don't actually help to develop your bike riding ability. They stop you from falling over and hurting yourself, which is not quite the same thing. Yes, they are a valuable stepping stone, but one that arguably takes you in the wrong direction before righting yourself. The stabilisers help to develop the confidence necessary to continue learning, but once the stabilisers are removed, there is a significant amount of readjustment required.

The dynamics between your body position, bike position, centre of gravity and propulsion are significantly different to the stabiliser phase. You have to unlearn what has got you thus far in order to readjust and progress to the next stage. We hate unlearning. It feels as though we are discarding the fruits of a considerable amount of time and effort (and sometimes money). These days, many children learn to ride a bike through using a preliminary 'balance bike' to try to negate the extent of unlearning required by the removal of stabilisers.

In short, we need to be confident learners and confident unlearners. Unlearning is not learning nothing; it's creating the capacity to move forward and reveal alternative avenues and directions. Unlearning is untying a knot ready for a new configuration.

Unlearning is essential for taking responsibility. Assessing what strategies have worked so far and what may be required in future requires another one of those honest conversations with yourself. Only you can come up with the answers, but more importantly, only you can derive the questions. In essence, you must consider when and how to graduate to your own personal balance bike. This is a question of the two selves: self-discipline and self-control. In other words, starting and stopping.

Progress is a tango between starting and stopping, toing and froing. Giving and taking sounds obvious enough, yet we are reticent to let things go. Once we've stumbled upon a strategy that seemingly works, it embodies our hard-won gains and we cherish it. The last thing we want to do is let it go; it feels like a backwards step.

Letting things go – slaying our darlings – can be the best but at the same time the hardest thing for us. We're used to questioning what doesn't work. Rarely do we question what does. Why would we? Life is lived by the mantra of 'if it ain't broke, don't fix it.' But as we know by now, growth is not polarised into convenient black and white extremes, but a hazy, fluctuating continuum requiring constant reassessment and re-evaluation. Cultivating the mental responsibility required to refine is essential if the numerous ups and downs are to be successfully navigated.

Things that work (to a degree) but might benefit from refining are often hidden in plain sight. Questioning that which hitherto we have had no cause to question (and perhaps even celebrated) is a good place to start. It might feel a little bit weird though, or even treacherous, as though we're betraying ourselves by even entertaining certain thoughts. Far from stabbing yourself in the back, however, you are simply performing personal due diligence and scouting for improvement opportunities.

Two key things to remember are:
1. The process is private (no one else needs to know what you're thinking), and
2. Asking a question is neutral. You are not casting aspersions.

Asking questions often becomes confused with making accusations. Indeed, asking a question can be an indirect way of making an accusation. A hypothetical question is a loaded statement. In the context of a programme of transformational resilience, however, we are interested in questioning ourselves and our environment for purposes of improvement. We mean well. Asking incisive questions is not meant to offend, although that doesn't mean people won't be offended. For this reason, I tend to keep the internal dialogue internal, until I see there is a genuine need for and benefit to sharing.

The questions asked are less about what is wrong but more about what can be further improved upon. It might sound like line-manager cliché, but in this instance, the sentiment is genuine.

> **Asking the questions doesn't mean your mind is made up. It means you are disciplined enough to remain open-minded.**

The more experienced we are, the more difficult it is to remain open-minded because of that build-up of accumulated experience. Our views become entrenched and compounded. In effect, taking responsibility is endeavouring to generate a fresh pair of eyes through which to see the world. To view things with unencumbered innocence – not sullied by our experiences – both good and bad.

Responsible questions might include:

The idea is to question the practices, attitudes and routines you've not thought to question previously – because you've had no cause to question them. We're universally preoccupied by the stuff that we suspect doesn't work. Sometimes the key to further improvement is hidden in plain sight. Substituting your stabilisers is the only way to move on. Shifting any single component of your improvement matrix has a knock-on effect on all the others, often enabling hitherto problematic elements to be tackled from new angles. Slithers of opportunity present between the shifting of your personal tectonic plates.

Stopping and starting

The stabiliser effect can be viewed in terms of personnel and resources. A company may lose a highly rated member of staff, changing the dynamic within the organisation. This subtraction can positively impact upon the workforce, providing new roles and opportunities for others to inhabit and make their own. These roles don't necessarily have to be formal; they can be subtle spaces for expressions of creativity, suggestion and camaraderie.

Traditionally, when a valued employee leaves a company, they can be described as a big loss to the establishment. With the right culture, however, it can provide a welcome boost to recalibrate and re-energise the existing workforce. Valuable capacity is created for others to grow into and inhabit. Without change, there is a risk of stagnation and complacency creeping in, regardless of good intentions. Doing the same thing over and over entrenches your behaviours. Even if what you are doing is right, should the winds of change blow, you become vulnerable and in no position to respond. And remember, the winds of change are always blowing.

Stopping and starting are the only initiatives required for improvement. They are the primary agents of change. Neither is more significant than the other. By asking yourself what you are going to start doing differently, or stop doing differently, all bases of change are covered.

You can stop doing unhelpful things or cease doing something that has worked thus far. Both create room for improvement. Starting to do something, or starting to do something differently, also generates potential for development. Some actions can be framed in terms of both stopping and starting. 'Starting to get 8 hours sleep a night' is aligned with 'stop staying up late'. But they're not quite the same, the sentiment is subtly different. The former is about betterment, the latter, damage limitation. Channelling resilience should always be about hoping for the best rather than fearing the worst.

Starting requires self-discipline: the ability to conjure new desired behaviours, routines and actions. This is a step into the unknown. At the outset, the intended results are always speculative and the rewards similarly questionable. A leap of faith is required. Self-discipline requires engaging with your inner maverick, finding your Han Solo.

On approaching the ominous and imposing Death Star, the reluctant hero and captain of the Millennium Falcon urges his co-pilot, Chewbacca, to 'fly casual'. Facing up to the unknown, flying directly into unchartered waters, Han understood the importance of 'faking it till you make it'. There is only one way to gain experience, which initially requires a certain degree of pretence or bravado. There is never a right time to start anything. By definition, you can never be fully ready to try something new, because you don't possess the requisite experience (or it wouldn't be 'new').

Actions not only speak louder than words, they must usurp them. In terms of acquiring experience, ultimately, the talking must end and the doing must commence. Self-discipline sometimes necessitates putting analysis on hold sufficiently long enough for the pursuit of credibility. Self-discipline is a voyage into the unknown with unpredictable consequences. Until the consequences become a little more predictable (and controllable), it is best to 'fly casual'.

Possible ways of flying casual:

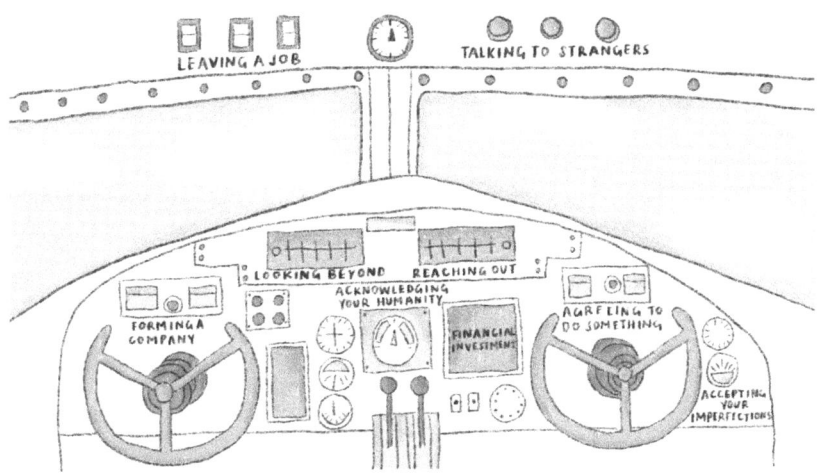

> **Self-discipline is the art of sustaining your starts. The longer you can keep on keeping on, the more chance you have of cultivating the resilience required to be the best that you can be.**

Sustained starting doesn't feel fresh and new after a while, so it pays to keep giving yourself gentle reminders about what you're doing and the reasons why. Once you get into the habit of 'flying casual' the persona becomes easier to adopt, and you approach the business of day-to-day with a can-do attitude. This in turn will start to bolster your inner Han Solo, and you realise that you can turn your hand to more and more with increasing success. You are acquiring experience.

Everythingism

Self-control is about putting a stop to things. Stopping is of equal importance to starting, if not more so. On some level, we all appreciate that we have to be selective. You can't do everything. 'Everythingism' is rife in society: most of us have a dose of it. Despite the multitude of technology and labour-savouring devices in our possession, we have more to do and less time to do it. We have the capacity to do three things at once and still try to do four. Thus, we do four things half as well, which, if my rudimentary maths serves me correctly, doesn't add up. 'Everythingism' has given us a high-tech plate, before proceeding to pile on way more than we can manage.

The question, therefore, is what are you going to discard?

E	X	H	A	U	S	T	I	O	N	V
X	N	O	T	C	O	P	I	N	G	N
U	N	H	A	P	P	Y	K	L	J	O
T	H	M	W	E	N	V	Y	F	H	T
I	N	D	E	C	I	S	I	O	N	I
S	Y	N	O	M	O	N	E	Y	G	M
F	O	R	G	E	T	F	U	L	Z	E

Self-control is the remedy to 'everythingism'. We spend our lives saying 'yes' (often despite our better instincts) when really, we should say 'no' to ourselves and others. Human beings are social animals – we need other people to interact with and live fulfilling lives. This often translates to 'people pleasing' behaviours and placating others at the expense of our own health and happiness. Consider how often you've reflected upon your day and cringed about your own personal policy of appeasement. We do ourselves down and big other people up when it is not warranted. We simply try to get through the day without making waves, generating inner turbulence instead. It's time to stop.

Stopping provides much needed space. Driving a wedge between what you routinely do and what you should (or more importantly shouldn't) be thinking, doing or saying, is the key to stopping. We possess a neural buffer zone, sandwiched somewhere between thoughts and actions, that has gradually concertinaed to be practically non-existent. This is your 'stop' zone, providing essential thinking time and space for reflection and consideration, rather than simply responding in knee-jerk fashion.

Human beings behave impulsively and emotionally. Admittedly, there is a time and a place for going with your gut instinct (such as avoiding that oncoming bus) but perhaps not all the time. Most everyday encounters require neither a fight nor a flight response. They require a more subtle, considered reaction.

Traditional received wisdom would have it that our worldly experience consists of contrasting events and their associated emotions. We process them through the filters of our temperament to decipher the best course of action. In short, our feelings inform the nature of our response. Feeling hot under the collar generates a different response to remaining cool, calm and collected.

However, scope for consideration exists between our experience of a particular event and the emotions we ascribe to it. The event itself is actually neutral, the importance and meaning we attach to it – our cognition – melds the subsequent emotion.

We are feeling our thinking.

The neutral world consists of …

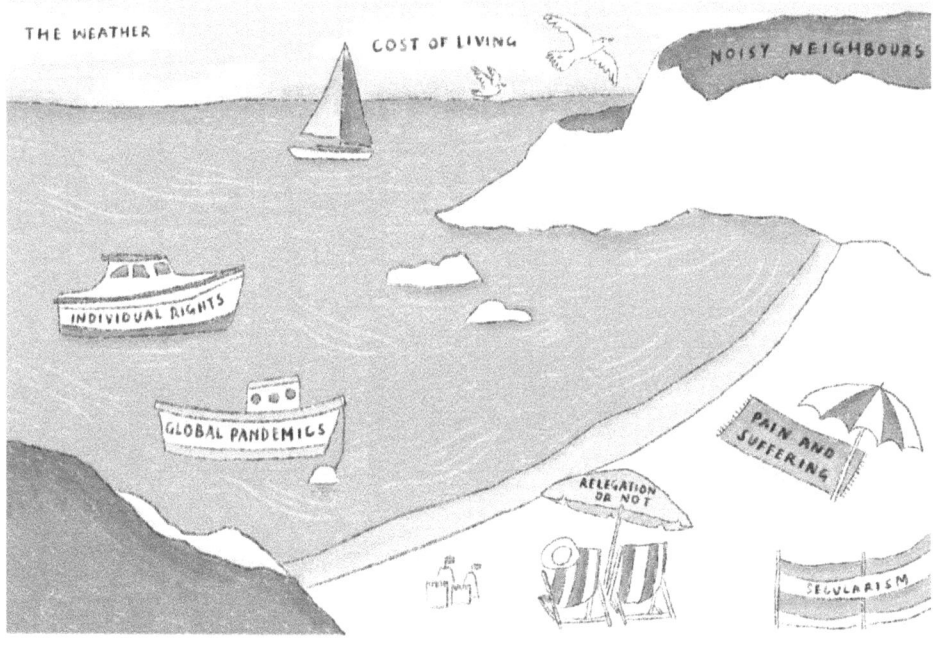

Whilst hard to believe at first, your feelings arise as a product of your thinking, not the other way around. There are a few physiological exceptions (such as feeling hungry) but, generally speaking, thoughts precede emotion, informing behaviour and resulting in outcome. You are largely the architect of how you perceive events, which subsequently colour your experiences of the world. Stopping, for a moment or two, enables you to take stock and create the space to consider the calibre of your thoughts.

Resilience 2.0: Embracing Challenge and Change

Creating space allows you to consciously invest your time and effort in the things that you want to, in a way that you want to, rather than being distracted by the agendas of others. Putting a stop to things is therefore not being negative and obstructive, rather selective. You are choosing how best to add value to your life. Without pausing, you will continue to spread yourself thinly and be of little benefit to yourself or others.

Stopping is best started sooner rather than later.

Some things to stop immediately:

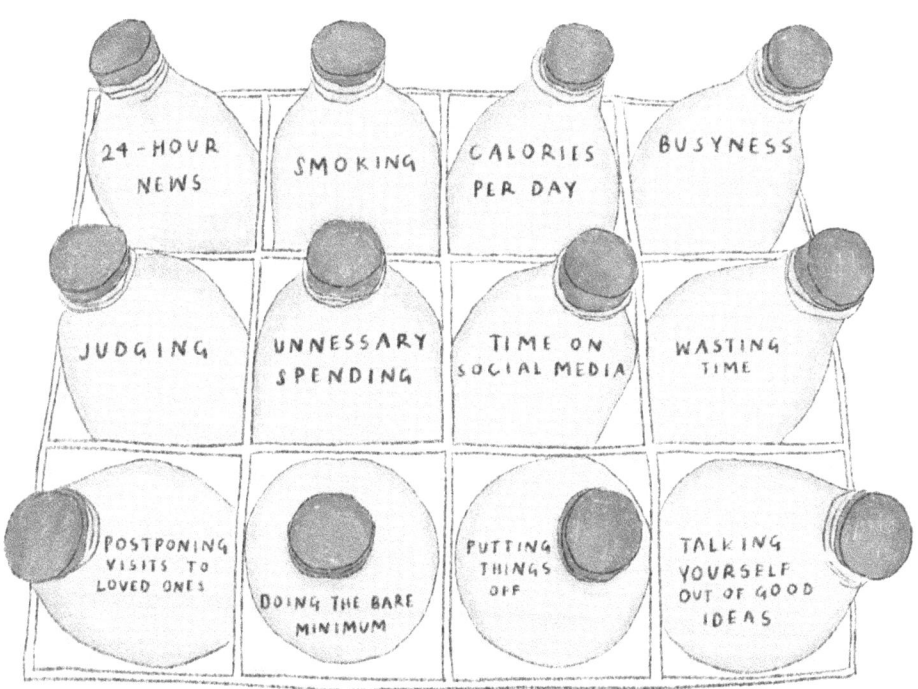

Guidance

Taking responsibility is essentially the art of stopping. From the moment we are born, we refine the relationship between our thoughts, actions and the environment we inhabit. We stop doing what we do and evaluate the alternative, before refining further. Trial and error repeatedly substitute what doesn't work, again and again, until it does.

Evolution relies heavily on our ability to continually refine. Rather than develop this capacity at school, we inadvertently learn to do the opposite. Refinement relies on making mistakes and responding accordingly. Education systems around the world put a premium upon avoiding mistakes, celebrating the achievement of the 'correct' pre-determined outcome in the shortest possible time. A race to the finish line does not always equip students with the means to stay ahead, however. Getting over the line doesn't mean you are fit for purpose.

> Some years ago, I travelled by car to a university I'd visited on several occasions. On this particular occasion, my phone had run out of battery power. I was left to navigate the remainder of the way by a mixture of memory and road signs. Needless to say, the journey wasn't straightforward. After more wrong turnings than I would have liked, I finally arrived at my destination via a rather circuitous and extended route. Late.

This episode serves as a metaphor for the value of engendering refinement. In schools, dedicated and well-meaning professionals are (often through no fault of their own) encouraged to operate like a classroom satellite navigation system. They show pupils exactly how to begin a task, the shortest and most direct route to completion, how to avoid any possible pitfalls, hold-ups and roundabouts, and the smoothest and most seamless journey. The teacher will warn the pupils at the earliest opportunity should they begin to deviate from the designated goal. Who can blame them? They don't have the time or space on the curriculum to do otherwise, being constantly

Resilience 2.0: Embracing Challenge and Change

judged upon how many children can be shepherded to the required 'destination'.

Perhaps an errant satnav would be more beneficial. Rather than continually showing pupils the right way to go, we should instead be inserting some additional obstacles and red herrings that promote responsible refinement. Instead of continually instructing pupils, we need to allow them the time and space to fathom what they should stop doing.

Stopping is not a passive pursuit; it requires conscious investment and endeavour. Human beings like to fill their time with stuff regardless of how useful that stuff is, in the hope that it creates substance. Substance – the things our lives consist of – can contribute to a sense of identity, which all of us secretly crave. An identity gives us meaning.

Unfortunately, if others can provide oven-ready pre-packed identities, we're prone to appropriation because it's easier. It's easier to look at someone else's answers rather than work it out for ourselves. Someone else's answers, however, may be right for them, but wrong for you. Because you are you, not them. Stop copying, start being!

Seeking meaning naturally draws you to like-minded individuals. Marketing campaigns fight to snare your attention and popularise certain thoughts, behaviours and beliefs. The successful promotions create a movement, endorsing and compounding views in an endless echo chamber. Unfortunately, this has a closing effect. Anyone with different views becomes an opposition, to be resisted and repelled as a challenge to your identity.

Closing is not the same as stopping. Closing is a narrow-minded unwillingness to engage with possibility. Stopping requires the most open of minds. It requires you to be more Bruce.

If you're not already aware, Bruce Lee was a legendary martial artist. If truth be told, there was probably more emphasis on the artist than the martial. He was an unconventional, uncompromising and creative innovator of a brand-new style of practice he christened Jeet Kune Do.

Only he wasn't. Jeet Kune Do wasn't a new style, at all. In truth, it wasn't even a style. Which is exactly the way Bruce wanted it. Confused? I'll explain.

Until Bruce came along, there was a lot of martial arts factionalism. Different forms of combat possessed their unique, identifiable traits and characteristics, with exponents of each style professing it to be better than the other. Bruce wasn't concerned by which style was the best. He was concerned with being the best, which is not quite the same thing. So, he came up with the concept of Jeet Kune Do. JKD was Bruce's practical manifestation of everything that the best styles were and everything they weren't. He was staunchly against a human trait commonly known as 'pigeonholing'. Pigeonholing refers to compartmentalising anything and everything into easily definable boxes, that fit comfortably within your current model of the world, but don't necessarily reflect the world.

Bruce realised the various styles of martial arts could not easily be categorised into separate clearly defined pigeonholes. There was too much overlap in terms of technique, application and effectiveness. Different martial arts were not actually… different. They were same-ish. They had good bits and bad bits and complementary bits. Pigeonholing them as this, that or the other didn't acknowledge the full extent of their qualities. Life, like Jeet Kune Do, has many overlaps and sometimes the edges are quite hard to distinguish. Rather than being preoccupied with defining edges, we should be broadening our horizons. We should be expanding our edges.

Bruce was keen to learn from anyone and everyone, anywhere and everything. It didn't make sense to pigeonhole, and assume the world is black and white when in reality it's technicolour. Jeet Kune Do is not actually a style at all, it's an all-encompassing physical manifestation of whatever works: an ante-style. As soon as it becomes defined by the parameters of a distinct, fixed identity, it's diversity and potential are curtailed – by becoming a 'thing' we automatically preclude anything and everything.

Taking personal responsibility requires active resistance to pigeonholing. It's easier initially to try to adopt a pre-existing identity and associated practices, but it's not quite you. Remaining open to what works and feels right is the only true path to being authentically you.

Personal responsibility requires remaining open-minded. It's easier to find what works for you – to find your true self – if you don't have other people's overbearing guidance getting in the way (however well-meaning). In the same way that 'a little information can be a dangerous thing', too much advice can be suffocating. Remember, you are not anyone else and never can be. Expending too much energy trying to imitate others is merely a distraction from finding your own unique identity. Besides, who wants to be a replica? You're an original.

Learning from others is invaluable, of course. That's very different to copying them. The former inspires inner growth, the latter is slapping on an external coat of gloss, an artificial veneer. To refine your potential requires the creative use of pre-existing ingredients to create something new. The new improved you.

Conscious struggle

Bruce had a simple way of assimilating good practice and experience with individual potential. He would continuously remind his pupils to engage in a four-step model of conscious struggle:

1. *Reflect honestly on your experiences: good, bad and indifferent*
   Invest equally in all aspects; don't overly dwell on the good or languish on the bad. Step outside of your emotions and observe the merits of what has and hasn't come to pass and the shifting dynamics between circumstance, actions and individuals. Consider the role of likelihood, luck and proximity, and the capacity for them to be repeated. Understand what can be understood and allow the rest to ferment. Sweep nothing under the carpet, indeed – keep everything on the table. Everything has value given the right situation at the appropriate time. In time, we will come to know the right time. Watch the constellations that present and wait patiently for those that don't. Eventually, they will, as night always follows day. The important thing is to be a regular observer, your own personal astronomer. In this way, your stars will align, and you will be alert to when.

2. *What does not work for you is of equal value to what does*
   Put simply, consider what hasn't gone well and endeavour to eliminate repetition in future. Avoidance may be all you need to successfully negotiate your goals. Crossing the road, for instance, is about selecting the gaps. It's not about the cars. Create the gaps and progress continues. Fixate upon the cars, and the obstacles remain ever-present. In pursuit of progress, it is human nature to add rather than subtract. There is a place for both construction and demolition of course, but the balance must be correct. Encouraging the gaps maximises breathing space: physically, intellectually and emotionally. You cannot do more if you are already exhausted. You cannot think clearly if you are constantly preoccupied. You cannot be motivated if you are mentally drained. Just as yin requires yang, something requires nothing.

3. *Endeavour to do more of the things that work for you*
   What has proven effective in the past is likely to work again. There is no limit to good news. Celebrate by repetition rather than

limitation. Rather than catastrophising, acknowledge that positive influences in your life multiply through interaction and application. Good things dwindle when levels of concentration slip. Remain focused. Pay homage to the positives in your life by living a positive life. Rather than exhausting your capacity to make good, you are your very own self-raising flour. Knead regularly to aerate. Fill your days with that which lifts you. Don't get stuck. Keep on keeping on.

4. *Explore new experiences to learn from*
    Actively seek that which you possess limited knowledge of. Regardless of right or wrong, engagement is nourishing. Experiences can be processed, deciphered, adopted or expelled: all of which are signposts on the righteous path. Life is not just about the cards you are dealt, but how you stick or twist. The more hands you play, the more skilful you become. Playing beats spectating. You cannot triumph from the sidelines, after all.

Remember: accepting responsibility is not about trying to be someone that you are not. Personal development is the art of accessing your potential. You're not trying to be someone different, just fulfilling what your life has to offer and your offer of life. You are mining your personal reserves. Improving yourself does not mean denying your identity. Self-improvement is about making more of your individual gifts and attributes, learning to identify with oneself more closely and working in harmony with your own particular configuration of genetics and circumstance. Learning is getting to know yourself better.

Your responsibility is to reveal what until now has lay hidden. Some people resist change because on some level they think it betrays who they are. This is somewhat to do with historical notions of class and system, where we have been encouraged to 'know our place' and ideas 'above our level' have been frowned upon. Your true identity comes about as a result of life's interactions. How you act, how you react, how you seek and how you find. The choices you make, and how the aftermath is woven. Proactively influencing your interactions is not a pretence, it is taking personal responsibility. Leaving your entire life's trajectory to the random and chance encounters initiated by others is surely a greater betrayal of your existence.

> **We are born and we die. Purpose is the bit in between.**

Listening to an account of Arnold Schwarzenegger's pathway into the movie business, I was struck as much by the interviewer's phrasing of the questions as I was by the responses. The Terminator was asked about a time he received lessons to dilute his distinct Austrian accent. Arnie was quick to discount this idea. Rather, he explained, the lessons were to help with formulating correct pronunciation. His articulation of some English language words rendered them unintelligible, or in some cases effectively changed the intended meaning. He was not changing his accent; he was just learning to enunciate words as they were intended to be spoken. Schwarzenegger's accent remained, but his grasp of speaking English improved.

The interviewer had slipped into the narrative of denial, implying Arnie's success was, in some part, due to disowning a part of who he was. In truth, he was simply educating himself in what he could do even better.

Some people may feel threatened by your journey of betterment. The realisation that there is an alternative does not sit comfortably with some, as they begin to ask painful questions of themselves. When questions are asked, they can be uncomfortable. The answers, even more so. People who truly care for you will embrace your endeavours. Those who do not, likely cherish an inhibiting narrative that has served them well thus far. Unconditional love is not reliant on limiting others.

You will likely already sense if such sentiments lace your current relationship(s).

Pace yourself

Whilst accepting responsibility takes effort, it should not be exhausting. Growth should be nourishing. The more you invest, the more energised you should feel. This requires pacing yourself. Moving too far too quickly, typically results in burnout and short-lived endeavour.

Carl Lewis won multiple Olympic gold medals. He was fleet of foot, which propelled him to victory in sprint events and long jumping. He was fast, very fast. In a race that regularly covered 100 metres in under 10 seconds, invariably it was Carl who was first past the post, often by some margin. His competitors trailed in his wake disconsolately, having strained every muscle and sinew in their body in a futile attempt to keep up. I guess you couldn't fault their effort.

In some ways, it might have been the effort that proved to be their undoing. Carl Lewis was fast. He was also relaxed. That didn't mean he didn't take his running seriously. Quite the opposite; he was a consummate professional. He realised that success is about doing what you do well to the very best of your ability. Sometimes, the effort to produce our very best can actually be counterproductive. If you push too hard, the pushing can have detrimental effects. Carl's fellow athletes tensed up in their competitive desperation to eke out a little more speed. In doing so, their form suffered and they actually lost speed. It may have felt like they were working hard to accelerate, but the result was the opposite of that which was intended.

Carl adhered to the 85% rule. He recognised that straining too hard loses more than it gains. Psychologically, it might feel like the right thing to 'give it your all' but this does not always translate to practical advancement. Refined struggle should always be concerned with making calculated improvement – which is sustainable improvement. Trying too hard too soon is the best way of burning out and prematurely giving in. Rather than always operating on the limit, dial it down to 85% of your maximum. You will be surprised how your level of performance will benefit from seemingly easing off the gas a little.

You will doubtless be surrounded by people who tend to dash around at 100 miles an hour like the proverbial headless chicken. They typically make a very public show of being extremely busy, and what is more, ensure everyone knows about it, lamenting their lot. The same people will be no more productive than anyone else, and in all likelihood less so. If they took an honest step back, quietly focusing on execution rather than elocution, they would no doubt be considerably more effective.

Your 15% discount boosts to productivity:

Your longevity depends upon your capacity to manage the volume of your output. Burnout is real and effects all of us, regardless of whether you are pursuing a congruent course of action or not. Operating at 85% also has the added benefit of helping you to consciously gauge what your maximum output might be. Indeed, it is wise to spend some time moving through your 'personal gears' now and then, making you mindful of the relationship between expenditure and reward. If you're constantly giving everything, it's hard to know your true value. Only by breaking your transactions down into incremental denominations can you gauge the full extent of your potential. Personal efficiency is key to planning your progress realistically, walking the fine line between that which is possible yet realistically achievable.

Naked ambition

Taking responsibility requires you to forge a truly individual path, leading rather than following. It's a potentially vulnerable time, as inevitably your actions gradually expose the true you. Your intentions, activities, behaviours and manner will align in the metamorphosis from intention to realisation. There is no hiding in a crowd of one. Such self-consciousness should not be confused with embarrassment. There is no shame in knowing yourself and acting accordingly. It is true bravery. No doubt some people will raise their eyebrows, but the majority will not. More than a few will be quietly in awe and secretly wishing they had done the same. It often takes one person to prove what is possible for others to follow. Personal responsibility blazes a trail.

Any nervousness and anxiety should be outweighed by a peaceful congruence, knowing that inwardly you are pursuing a course of growth and starting to realise your true potential. In doing so, you are likely expunging the collateral damage acquired through years of doing things as others see fit. Ultimately, the closer you can get to behaving in keeping with the real you, the better for you (and those who genuinely care for you).

Privately, we're accomplished at doing the things we want to do, when left to our own devices. Our priorities are crystal clear; we know what we desire and behave accordingly. Whilst we may have to juggle the practicalities of work or family commitments, when presented with one of those blissful (albeit rare) opportunities to do as we please, we do just that.

You don't pretend you're someone else. You pursue your pursuits and enjoy doing what you enjoy doing. You become markedly less self-conscious and inwardly drop the pretence. There is no time that you are more authentic than when left alone to the sanctity of your own devices. You are good company for you, if stripped of the oppressive weight of external expectation and responsibility.

You are, of course, still beholden to you. This does not feel like a mental burden, however, just an integral part of your psyche. Rather than lugging around someone else's cumbersome baggage, responsibility to yourself is beautifully, evenly distributed throughout your whole being, perfectly balanced and aligned. You acquire no personal blisters through wearing an ill-fitting life. You are who you want be, living the life you want to lead. You are living. You are fulfilled.

> **Your public persona should feel the same as your private orientation. The greater the disconnect, the more uncomfortable you will likely feel – physically, emotionally and spiritually.**

The more you refine your thoughts and actions to align with your inner calling, the freer and more energised you become. Worry less about what others might think of you. Most will think nothing. Those who judge merely reflect their own insecurities. Your authentic pursuit magnifies their emptiness; those who live pointless lives quickly try to shift the focus elsewhere, for the comparison is difficult to dwell upon. Instead, worry about what you think. You don't really have a choice but to follow your calling. Everything else is just background noise, the static of life, which only clouds your understanding and muffles your appreciation. The more your path is refined with honesty and personal integrity, the clearer it becomes, the more straightforward it is to follow. There are less distractions and fewer incidental dramas. The main players become less significant and your own life falls into place.

Your own life holds so much more promise than you realise. As we grow older, we tend to consign our dreams to naïve childhood enthusiasm. The once abundant potential for excitement and enthusiasm is swamped by a preoccupation with paying the mortgage. We substitute emotion with going through the motions. Where once we dared to dream, we neither dare nor dream. By the age of seven years old, we are already beginning to ring fence our lives. We emulate society when society doesn't work. We pretend to be anyone but ourselves, fearful of our own limitations. Before leaving school, we have long since learnt what we cannot do, who we cannot be and how we cannot behave. We have learnt not to learn.

Ultimately, to become truly resilient, we need to **redefine** what we are capable of.

Chapter 14

Redefining

I wouldn't say that many of the notions you hold about yourself are a lie. But neither are they entirely true.

Think about it. Where does the substance of your character come from? What makes you lousy at mathematics or a competent pianist? Why do you treat people like you do? What has led you to your current occupation or preoccupation? How did you end up where you are, doing what you do, with the people you are with? What leads you to be a good dad, a lousy uncle, a considerate partner or a self-centred egotist? What leads you to believe you are a good dad, a lousy uncle, a considerate partner or a self-centred egotist?

Opportunity knocks

Talent, opportunity, circumstance and genetics have all played a significant part. But none more so than chance. By some sort of serendipitous configuration, the stars have aligned to create the life you are now living. For better or for worse, you are a product of umpteen rolls of the dice in a universal game. The dice may or may not be weighted, but they've been rolled all the same.

You are a real-life Monopoly piece, possibly going round and around the same old streets, chancing your luck and rarely passing Go. Things could have been so very different, of course. There are almost infinitesimal alternative configurations of you in parallel universes. If only you had chosen differently, you would have different choices.

But you *still* have choices.

You can deviate from your individual chosen path and make your own way, just like you always could. Nothing has changed in that sense.

You are no more or less limited than you have ever been. You may think you are, of course, and therein lies the source of the limitation. Thoughts undermine our actions. Our judgements are made through mental construct and projection rather than the actual. We don't do it because we think we can't do it. We don't leave because we think we won't be able to. We don't start a 'start-up' because we're not sure that it will work. We don't bother to ask questions of ourselves because we're afraid we might not be able to find the answers. We don't look, we don't try, just in case we are found wanting. In case. So, we settle for being unsettled in a world of ever-decreasing circles, hiding from today whilst being afraid to seek out tomorrow.

Your limitations are not you. Your limitations are potential consequences that you project into your consciousness. They are you in a galaxy a long time ago, far, far away. We ward off our futures simply because there is a version that might not work out. That's true, of course. There are many different unsatisfactory ways that your life can play out. Sometimes they actually come to pass. Sometimes.

Most of the time, they don't. The worst thing that can happen rarely does. Self-limiting your ambition and curtailing your future doesn't actually prevent the hurt. The worst things still happen to the best of us.

The best things also happen to the worst of us.

Sometimes there is no rhyme or reason to how fate plays out. Maybe even most of the time. Pretending there is clouds the possibility of a better future. We dwell upon the risks, we fixate upon the downsides and we belittle our futures. We do a good job of manifesting the bad: of becoming our own self-fulfilling prophecies and harbingers of daily doom. Slowly but surely, we incrementally grind ourselves down, carrying the weight of what might come to pass in a worst-case scenario. Our tomorrows are tainted long before they dawn.

We learn from an early age to know our place, acknowledge our limitations and punch below our weight. The chances are you're not surprised by your circumstance. You may feel an ache of disappointment, but neither is your current predicament news to you. For good or for bad, our lives seem to fit us. Many of us do not have the luxury of regret; the missed opportunities and alternative choices seemingly never presented themselves. There were no glass slippers, no beanstalks, no frogs to kiss and no ivory towers. You were never in the fairy tale. Your story was always one of getting by, probably for as long as you can remember. Of survival.

From the cradle to the grave, you take on the role of you. Your unscripted improvisation falls within the remit of your characterisation, as the things that 'could only happen to you', indeed, happen to you. Funny, that. Those events and circumstances you often become embroiled in are just the sort of unlikely coincidences you've come to expect.

The truth? They are no coincidence.

There might be an element of fortune or misfortune, but the defining trajectory of our life follows an undefined groove within which we predominantly fluctuate. We have ups, downs and deviations, but only within the narrow parameters of our adopted limitations. In a world of opportunity, we rarely venture outside the borders of familiarity. Repetition of unthinking thought, word and action entrenches our behaviour and confines our ability to think beyond the past and look to the future.

When you were a small child you asked, 'what if?' Now you don't even ask. We accept the unacceptable, endure the uncomfortable, humour injustice and perpetuate a life of unfulfillment.

And then you die.

My question is, what are you going to do about it?

Start by *redefining* you.

> **You are not forever consigned to be a victim of personal circumstance. The stars can, indeed, realign. But you do have to look to the stars to acknowledge it. Look up, rather than down. To the future rather than the past.**

Age is no barrier to change. Neither is circumstance. Whilst both will likely present practical questions, the answers can be found when there is a genuine desire. For those viewing the world with a cynical hangover borne through experience, your options are not limitless. There will, indeed, be things that are beyond you, goals that cannot be scored, dreams that may not manifest and yellow brick roads that don't actually lead anywhere.

But nothing has changed in that respect.

Genetics have always precluded us from reaching some pinnacles and accelerated us towards others. There are only ever a handful of people who achieve the ultimate. There is only one Olympic 1500m gold medallist. But that doesn't mean you can't be in the race, or some other race, and succeed. Success means different things to different people, all equally valid. Only you know what it looks like for you. The question marks that remain over the full extent of your potential shouldn't stop you from asking the questions. They shouldn't curtail your appetite or quest for growth and improvement.

Upgrading resilience requires comparison with yourself rather than critical relativism. Rather than being deterred by the likelihood of scaling the highest summits, or fearful of sinking into the deepest valleys, we should enjoy exploring the landscape and traversing the slopes. There are endless paths to be taken, numerous rises and falls and ample adventures to be had. You don't have to be the very best in the world to be your best. But you have to get out there, which probably means exiting the historical confines of your mind.

Redefining how you see yourself and the world is key to opening up a world of enormous possibility. Your view of the world is what makes your world. The material substance of our daily events has no meaning until we apportion some sort of value or worth, which subsequently manifests into feelings. If we change the way we look at things, the things we look at change. Shifts in paradigm can shake up our world. Redefining requires entertaining a very different perspective. Most of us only entertain small-scale difference. What's needed is a cognitive revolution: a popular uprising of your mind.

It is possible to see things completely differently. To find something that hitherto has remained hidden from mental view. In terms of incremental improvement, you've become adept at managing your current circumstances. Redefining involves supercharging your competence to master further realms of possibility.

> There are far-flung villages in the remotest of places that can now access the internet. A world of opportunity has been remotely opened up. People can connect, learn, interact and experience new horizons, shaking-up their existing view of the world. The world is now a very different place for those villagers. Most of the change has not taken place materially, however. Broadly speaking, the village still looks the same. The real shift has taken place within the mind. Wifi has introduced a world of possibility and expanded horizons. The world is somehow the same but different. The change is huge – and it's happened on the inside. From the outside, the village – and the villagers – appear the same.

Your world can change now if you're prepared to entertain the possibility of discarding your darlings, ridding yourself of those familiarities that you have harboured and held dear for so long. We become attached to debilitating thoughts about our own place in the world, just because they are 'our' thoughts. We might not like our identity (and be acutely aware of it) but it's better than being a no one. We can bear anything apart from being invisible.

Redefine who you are. Discard the limitations that have curtailed your future and dulled your days.

You can still aspire. You can still enjoy. You can still learn. You can still get excited. You can deviate. You can differ. You can break out. We're dismissive of possibility whilst rarely experiencing or even engaging. Without action you can truly never know. Throw off the shackles of everything you've come to dislike about yourself and start to change the narrative.

You are far more capable than you think.

Acting your shoe size

Ageing does not mean you have to grow old. Whilst none of us are getting any younger, that doesn't mean we have to blindly accept physical and mental limitation and deterioration. Yet, we do. We stop playing and grow old. In truth, we grow old because we stop playing. We reach a certain age and feel compelled to act like it, as though we have to usher in an inevitability. Alternatively, I've always been an advocate of acting your shoe size not your age.

We can continue cultivating our health and fitness, maintaining active, fulfilling lifestyles until the very end. I'm not just talking about a sedentary walk around the garden, either. Unless you are/were a professional athlete, I believe it's possible to be fitter and stronger than you've ever been until a very ripe old age. You don't actually know what you're capable of because you have never really pushed yourself. We're dismissive of our potential. It is possible to have both quality and quantity of life. You just need to challenge the narrative:

* When you've had enough, you can always manage more
* When you've reached the end of your tether, it's not actually the end
* When you don't know what to do, you actually have some inkling
* When you've exhausted all the options, there are still some remaining
* When you've run out of time, you can make time
* When you're tired, you are not too tired
* When it's too late, it isn't
* When the sun sets, the day isn't over
* When you're lost for words, you can find them
* When you can't go on, you can
* When there's nothing else for it, there is always something else
* When there's nowhere left to turn, keep turning
* When it's not meant to be, it's simply not the case.

Redefining what 'is' and what 'isn't' meant to be is the gateway to genuine lasting change. Human beings are capable of amazing things but we have to get out of our own way. This sounds straightforward, but, of course, the reality is far from it. The gateway doesn't always have a whole lot to do with reality.

Narnia thinking

C S Lewis' book, *The Lion the Witch and the Wardrobe*, treads a beautiful and poignant dalliance between fact and fiction, blurring the lines between the real and imaginary. It's a filter that most of us use on a daily basis. Experiences are processed, embellished, and amended by the black box between our eyes, to project the life we believe we inhabit. The real world may be all around us, but it's piloted from the confines of a neural cockpit. We never actually set foot into the world.

It's viewed instead, second hand, from behind our curated human barricades. We can never fully rid ourselves of the barricades, but we can become more permeable, allowing real-world experiences to flow more easily with less evolutionary and sociological moraine. Your experience of life can be closer to the truth.

In Lewis' literary classic, four wartime evacuees discover an imaginary world, accessed via a fur-coated portal at the back of a wardrobe. Lucy, Peter, Susan and Edmund undertake all sorts of adventures and struggle to overcome the oppression of the White Witch. Narnia is quite a place, a place of magical intrigue, danger, friendship, liberty and hope.

The children become gradually aware of a long-standing legend, prophesizing the arrival of the new King or Queen of Narnia. Legend has it, that any day now, Royalty will return and provide salvation from the clutches of the evil queen. It's expected to be quite an occasion, and the children are eager to bear witness to it. Despite the rumours, however, there is no sign of the heir to the throne, and the children begin to feel increasingly disillusioned by the no-show.

Finally, Aslan the lion, an all-seeing omnipotent prescient character, has a quiet word. The four young protagonists have consistently shown courage, bravery and integrity. They have repeatedly demonstrated their credentials to lead. Evidently, the children are the new Kings and Queens of Narnia. They are the chosen ones that legend has foretold. The children are, in effect, waiting, for their own arrival.

Lucy, Peter, Susan and Edmund are typical of the way human beings manage to hide from themselves in plain sight. Despite possessing ample portions of the right stuff, they still viewed themselves in the same way that they had always done. Despite evidence to the contrary, in their own eyes, they were just some kids that had been evacuated. They were perennially the pre-wardrobe kids.

Most of us remain pre-wardrobe kids and never return to claim our thrones. It's time that all of us came out of the closet. Redefining requires us to visualise our future rather than rehash the past, acknowledging the reality of now and relinquishing the baggage of then. The old you is not always a friend of the new you, and likely has, at times, something of a strained relationship with the current you.

The past is not an impediment. It has been and gone. If you so choose, you are able to move on, guilt-free. It makes no sense to anchor your self-worth in historical circumstance. Ask why you view yourself in the way you do; there will be little rational 'reason'. Much of the 'evidence' will relate to something that happened long ago. Times change, people change, so give yourself a break. The real you is the current you, not a residual memory of once-upon-a-time.

Assess your actions and behaviours of the everyday. They are the constituent components of the person who you truly are, right now.

You are the product of:

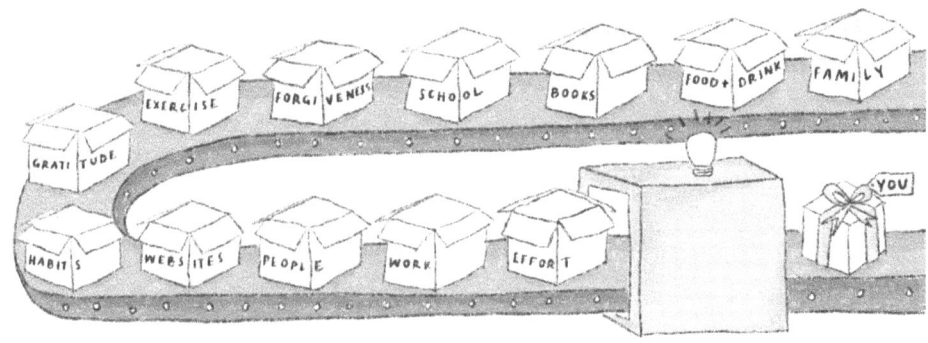

Resilience 2.0: Embracing Challenge and Change

Everyday resilience

In practice, daily resilience entails making the right choices every day. Your choices both make you and define you. The sum of small choices combine to make a big difference. The beauty of such seemingly insignificant choices is that they are so abundant and numerous that there is something for everyone. They can be started today. Right now, in fact. Indeed, when determining to change, determining is the key component. Once the shift begins, a momentum is created that helps facilitate wider change.

I remember a friend of mine proudly regaling the fact that he was a 'weekend warrior'. His weekends consisted of all manner of physical endeavours and challenge, extreme or otherwise. He truly made the most of his weekends and thrived in the contrast between the two days of concentrated activity and his predominantly sedentary working lifestyle.

After a little reflection, both of us wondered whether his life would be enhanced further from aspiring to be more 'weekday warrior' as well as 'weekend warrior'. His weekends were effectively compensation for the majority of his life. A life pursuing compensation is not ideal. A life pursuing a life, is surely infinitely more rewarding. Living for the weekend is capping your expectations at around 29% of your potential.

Embracing resilience requires accessing 100% percent of you. Rather than resigning ourselves to making the best of a bad job, of living small, we need to redefine what we want from our lives and where we see our place within that. Your place should be in the centre, or at least not far off. You should be in the driving seat.

Forget you not

From time to time we attend a service of remembrance, thanksgiving or even a celebration. A time that is scheduled into the diary to bring people together and mark a particular event, those involved, and perhaps the sacrifice, commitment and dedication displayed. Some of these events are sacrosanct. Depending upon the nature of the occasion, a whole country will effectively pause their daily business and take time to remember.

Some occasions are actually billed as festivals of remembrance.

We are effectively remembering to remember.

Which makes me wonder what we do in the intervening periods. Perhaps we forget the enormous promise of our lives. Something worth acknowledging is surely worth placing front and centre of our consciousness. We forget until we are reminded to remember, which means we forget who and what we are, and our responsibility to ourselves.

Redefining requires taking careful, purposeful steps to keep yourself front and centre. Rather than reserving your best life for the weekend, it should permeate your weekstart and weekmiddle. Eating healthily on a Monday and Tuesday won't compensate for binging and over-indulgence from Friday to Sunday. A walk through the park once a week doesn't constitute a healthy lifestyle. Registering for Spanish classes on the 1st of January doesn't make you a linguist. You cannot compartmentalise resilience, dabbling one day and reverting back to old ways on another.

Rather than changing your behaviours, you are required to change you. Viewing yourself as someone who makes the right choices about food is far more powerful than someone who jumps on the latest dietary bandwagon. Instead of taking Spanish lessons you are a language student. The difference may sound simply semantic, but the effect is far more profound. True change requires a shift in persona, in identity. It requires becoming the person that you want to be, someone who

Resilience 2.0: Embracing Challenge and Change

inhabits and embodies the practices and routines required to create meaningful and lasting change. You have to become that person: you. This is not the same as being someone who embarks upon a new venture and has 'all the gear but no idea'. The trappings of a new hobby display an outside-in approach to growth. Whilst some new equipment may be required, it must not be utilised to compensate practical investment (or lack of). Most New Year's Resolutions fail precisely because they are a bolt-on ritual, ushering the end of the festive season. When the New Year ceases to be new, they lose relevance – along with mince pies, Christmas crackers and pine trees. The only way to master change is to be the change that you want to see.

You are not a temporary act of remembrance. Your life should pay homage to you. Not in a selfish, self-centred narcissistic way, but quite the opposite. By making the most of your unique strengths, talents and attributes, you are exercising the potential you have been given, rather than inflating what you haven't. This may have been provided by God, the universe or a chance biological encounter, but you have been endowed with huge promise, nevertheless. We all come and go. Anyone and everyone who has ever lived, will also die. The bit that matters is the filling in between. This is your calling: your purpose, your vocation. This is you. The sooner you can find yourself the better. You will know when you have found your true vocation; there will be an inner peace and contentment. It will feel like you're finally home.

Happiness should not be confused with placation. Getting by is often merely papering over the cracks. Short-term fixes help from one day until the next without really changing anything for the better, and often make things worse. We seek without ever really finding.

Genuine happiness and contentment is derived from the pursuit of meaning, engaging in whatever it might be that aligns with your aspirations, abilities and desire. Defining that purpose is key, otherwise the direction you're heading in will be wayward, unrewarding and potentially destructive. Redefining means taking an honest look at your place in the world and considering how you've arrived there. Is it by default or design? Are you living a life that you want to lead or merely settling for the convenience of the company you keep? If it's the latter, let me assure you that you are far from alone. If your Spidey-sense is tingling, trust your intuition. You cannot change what has already come to pass, but you sure as hell can take back control of your life. Today.

Remember that upgrading resilience is not a passive pursuit. Indeed, a passive pursuit does not actually take you anywhere due to your passivity. Passive pursuers don't actually go after anything; they wait for good things to come to them. Sometimes they strike lucky, of course, most of the time they don't. Redefining requires you to constantly be on your toes, considering whether the choices you make are actually your choices, or simply indulging someone else's.

> **Only by staying on your toes do you stand a chance of reaching higher.**

It requires effort, it requires balance and it requires practice. Sometimes it requires learning and sometimes it requires unlearning. Moving from surviving to thriving is a stretch. Flexibility of mind and body is key.

Chapter 15

Blaze a Trail

There are some very remote, inhospitable and inaccessible places on this planet. Some of them are cold and some of them are hot. The Maasai Mara is one such place, a vast national game reserve in Kenya, sprawling over 1,500 square kilometres. It's home to a rich assortment of wildlife – a truly A-list supporting cast of lions, tigers, wildebeest, hippos, elephants… a comprehensive who's who of jungle movers and shakers.

An integral part of the community is an exclusive group of human 'intuitives', charged with tracking down the whereabouts of some of the main players. Keeping tabs on the animal kingdom is not always easy – often far from it. Tracking requires bottling the essence of passage, capturing clues as to possible whereabouts and piecing together prediction. It involves assimilating a journey to derive a likely destination. In short, what has been suggests what is to come.

Clues consist of identifying subtleties that would escape the majority of us. A broken twig here, a scuffed riverbank there, a scattered flock, an interested third party. The signs are hard to spot and even harder to decipher direction from. Yet to the trained eye, they are accurate indicators of a wild animal's passage. Some natives of the Maasai Mara have dedicated a lifetime to reading the wilderness and interpreting the subtleties of changing environment.

Making your mark

Take a moment to track your life. Without apportioning judgement, choices, events and circumstances have all led you to this point and juncture in time. It might be a fair reflection of your efforts and endeavours and, just as likely, it may be a complete and utter travesty. Life is not fair, much as we'd like to think the opposite is so, however much we encourage our children to believe that we live in a meritocracy. Bad things happen to good people and vice-versa. Again and again. But believe me, you don't have to remain a victim and accept that your entire life's path is predetermined.

There is no inevitability.

Whilst you can track your past – the scuff marks, the pivotal changes of direction and choices that shaped your bearing – it does not automatically define your destiny. Regardless of your current predicament and circumstance, it does not have to be tomorrow's current predicament and circumstance. At its core, resilience empowers change. We can all, every single one of us, learn to be better. We can elevate our lives from a humdrum daily struggle for survival to a thriving, more promising future for ourselves and our families. Your previous misdemeanours, your unpleasant encounters and buried trauma can be banished to the vanguards of personal history as you implement a programme of change for the better. For your betterment. Your tracks will follow wherever you choose to lead.

Some of your footsteps can be retraced should you so desire; sometimes it pays to revisit and make good previous misadventures. There is never a right time to make things right, just so long as you make time. It is possible to right wrongs.

If at first you don't succeed? Then you are human. Each and every one of us is an extended collection of misdemeanours, mishaps and miscalculations. How you respond, and how often you are prepared to evaluate and re-evaluate your responses, is the only thing that separates success from failure. Evolutionary neurological circuitry constantly urges us to put our feet up; suggesting we should rest. Settle. We've done enough for today. In a time when survival was for the fittest and resources seemed scant, Mother Earth was keen that we preserved our energy and reserved our efforts for when called upon. Survival was a careful balancing act between channelling effort and damming life force. We never expended more than we had to. Staying alive took all we had.

You are more than heartbeats, respiration and preservation, however. You are the personification of a question with the ability to manifest answers. And if you don't like the answers? Then you can ask different questions and find alternative ways and means to create a congruent future. It is never, ever, too late. You will find no peace in a begrudging acceptance of unrequited living, instead harbouring a hot dissatisfaction that infiltrates both day and night. You lie awake in the dark and lethargy dulls your waking hours.

> **Take steps. As soon as you make strides, you make progress.**

There is nothing that cannot be reversed. Debts can be addressed, careers can be altered, relationships rekindled or terminated. Ill health does not have to define you, rather choose to do what you will with the time you have available. For those are the very same choices we all wrangle with. Yet the choices we make are limited. We tinker with the minutiae of our day, rarely venturing from the familiarity of engrained routine, seeking solace in the unsurprising and uninspiring.

You are bigger than that. You are worth more than that. Regret is the final dish served upon your last supper. By then, it's too late to reorder. Now is the time to put your life in order. If work isn't working, you can work it out. If home is not where the heart is, it's time to move. If you feel like an imposter, get to know the real you. If you have difficult questions to address, first enquire of yourself then share with others. Honour your existence. Value you. Resilience 2.0 is the best of you:

a wake-up call and reminder of your beautiful, unique, precious individuality.

Resilience 2.0

Receptivity is the restoration of an ability to dream once more. For those of us who have forgotten how to daydream, the spark needs to be rekindled. Those very same dreams contain the creativity and imagination that illuminate your potential. Life isn't dull, only the blinkered people within it: the supporting cast who bemoan their lot whilst doing nothing to rectify it. Be open once more. Pursue until barriers present and then overcome them. The insurmountable is rarely insurmountable, and usually negotiable. If time is your obstacle, then consider how you want to spend that time: in creating something better or resenting that you didn't?

> **There really is no choice but to believe in you. If you don't, few others will. Believe. Then be.**

Risk is non-negotiable. You cannot choose to circumnavigate risk, only to meet it headlong with courage and bravery, or run from it. Running is futile. It will always catch up with you in the end. Risk is an ever-present adversary, whispering negativity and naysaying, constantly belittling your actions and aspirations. It can only be slayed by direct action – tamed by fronting up to your own insecurities. For it is only your insecurities – only you – that fuels the dragon which heralds from within. There will be those around you who stoke the dragon's ire under the guise of well-meaning friendly advice. Genuinely well-meaning friends will support your journey. The positive change will be evident and the benefits even more obvious. Those who stand in your way stand for nothing.

> **Be respectful and mindful of all but do not compromise your life. Stand tall, aim high, dream big and bring it on.**

Take a stand for your standards, for they are worth fighting for. They form the backbone of your existence. Without them, you can never hold your head high.

The real risk is not to live. To breathe, to pulse but never truly feel alive. Do not waste your existence. Exist loudly, brightly and unashamedly. Apologise to no one for being you. Hold yourself accountable and be prepared to take a leap. Life is not for shrinking. Find yourself and fortune favours the brave. Success is never judged from the outside. It joins your inner dots, making you feel complete. Entering the fray is victory in itself. You feel something. You feel alive.

Retention is the key: what separates the realisation of dreams from a relapse into the old ways. Most of us begin with noble intentions and a fire in our belly. We all promise ourselves that 'this time' it will be different. Realise this: your life is neither fashion nor fad. Quick fixes rarely hold, novelty soon wears thin and surfaces will inevitably tarnish. Character, however, remains rich and does not diminish. Stay true to your core and you will stay the course. Value your purpose and your purpose will increase in value. Knowing that there will be times when progress is negligible, your efforts seem futile and your hard work is seemingly in vain, is valuable preparation. That is when you will start to make a difference. Know this: you will eventually get there. You will eventually make it. If you live and breathe the change that you truly want to see, it will happen. It may not take the form that you originally envisaged, for the journey often amends the outcome, but the result will be overwhelmingly positive, nonetheless. An infinitely better place awaits, regardless of that which you currently inhabit.

Stick at it. Stay on target. Be relentless. Be selfish in your single-minded pursuit. Be bloody-minded and do not deviate when you know that your track is the right track. Do not be easily swayed or carefully persuaded. There are only a few who truly retain. There is no rhyme or reason why it can't be you. You are the defining factor. You determine to stay determined or fall by the wayside. You. If you get this, you've got this. Spend your time rather than fritter your days. Measure your progress by concerted application rather than casual clock watching. Your life is no pretence.

> **The sands of time may indeed run, but if you remember to continually turn, you are solely in charge of your destiny. It's down to you – or perhaps more importantly – up to you.**

Honestly? Responsibility cannot be found in a book. It cannot be 'liked' online or signposted via a #hashtag. It cannot be discovered, stumbled upon, replicated or reviewed. Responsibility cannot be bought or sold or begged or borrowed. It comes from within. It is part of your DNA. You are biologically and genetically predisposed to function the way you do. Accepting responsibility requires the courage to get out of your own way and reveal your inner workings and machinations. Do not hinder yourself. Rather than being bowed by expectation or convention, see once again with the eyes of a child and feel unapologetically.

Strip away the layers of incidental complexity that have accumulated from years of distraction. Keep things simple. Celebrate your differences, for there really is no one like you. No one in this world walks in your shoes or dances to your rhythm. Only you can put your finger on what it means to be you. Find this, hold on tightly with all your might. Do not let go of that which makes you feel alive. For it is precious: the essence of you. Once you've found your thing then roll with it through storms and still waters. Remember, your course will require many adjustments so remain steadfast at the helm. Sometimes you will have to tack into the wind, sometimes away.

Resilience 2.0: Embracing Challenge and Change

> **Progress is sometimes short but usually long, but it is progress, nevertheless. A year from now you'll be glad you took action. A day from now you will be glad you took action.**

Regularly revisit what you are about. Remind yourself. Tweak your days and your nights, nudge your thoughts and practices and tame your mental meanderings. Corral your intentions.

Redefining is both the beginning and the end of the journey. Transformation cannot begin without some inkling of the existence of another way. An acknowledgement and admittance that there's more to it than this. A question mark. A redefining cannot be completed without embracing change with the whole of your being. When it is done, you will be a different being to the one currently underpinned with angst and self-doubt. Emotions buried deep may well need to be exhumed – a messy affair – but essential, nonetheless.

You must see yourself in a different light. You must see yourself in light, rather than permanently masked in the semi-umbra of circumstance. There is no circumstance beyond your control, there is always a slight adjustment to be made, steps to be taken, something that can be done. You can always make a start, however small. A small step underpinned with authentic intention belies its magnitude. Nudging is the beginning of the story – a catalyst for the story. And the beginning is the most important part, for most never even turn the front cover. Most are scared to acknowledge there is a story that they are worthy of starring in. We scan the back covers of other people's lives, thinking 'that would be nice. If only…'

You are worthy. Your story awaits and it's not an obituary. Only you can narrate it. It lies unwritten, but the blank pages are most definitely there. If you don't make your mark someone else will, in a hand pretending to be yours, telling a tale in another scripture. You have to make your mark.

> **Know this: you enter and exit by the stage door. At least set foot upon the stage.**

We are – all of us – constantly redefining our limitations. Like pebbles on a beach, the tumultuous spray of existence crashes continuously, moulding our self-worth through the relentless attrition of society's expectations.

Prioritise your expectations. Raise your expectations. Learn to be better and get better at learning.

At living.

Because in the end, the life you live is the life you make.

Make it a good one.

Embrace change.

Rise to the challenge.

Up your resilience.

You 2.0.